Conversational Musicology:

a composer's perspective

Rosemary Mountain

CONVERSATIONAL MUSICOLOGY: a composer's perspective

Second edition: October 31, 2024.

First published January 2021.

ISBN: 978-1-7774836-1-6

Published by R. Mountain

www.armchair-researcher.com

Cover art by the author.

Conversational
Musicology:

a composer's perspective

TABLE OF CONTENTS

IV. Transmission Among Scholars & Artists

V. Other Topics for Reflection

Rosemary Mountain

PREFACE

This book has various purposes:

- to present some personal observations, reflections, and convictions about music - its nature & its participants;

- to reflect on the diversity of ways in which people encounter music, interact with it, and express their reactions to it;

- to comment on potential imbalances in priorities of music training and research;

  and

- to argue in favour of re-instating more casual forms of research communication within music and cognate disciplines, and to accept recognition of the individual transmitter's voice and discipline as a supplement to existing research traditions.

Conversations about music will almost always involve different perspectives, simply because music has so many different facets and participants. Many who are involved in such conversations seem unaware of the sheer multiplicity of perspectives possible. This is particularly true of those who restrict their talking about music to specialized environments: conferences, classrooms, and social meetings with friends (often chosen precisely due to shared preferences and aversions). This book outlines an imagined future where diversity of perspectives might be more easily identified, respected, and balanced. A main argument is that the world of music research could benefit from more climates and environments where we can discuss – passionately if we wish, or haltingly, or obliquely, or playfully – any aspect of music and related issues.

In an effort to be concrete, I have organized the book into topics to highlight and acknowledge different approaches, and to provide some context for these differences. I also propose (in cursory fashion) a few strategies for more articulate cross-disciplinary conversations. I had originally hoped that this book might turn out to be useful for students at senior undergraduate

i

levels, and for young faculty members wishing for some arguments (or at least sympathy) to help effect changes in curricula, or to identify potential areas and strategies for research - although I am aware that the old-fashioned style of prose or the overly-subjective flavour of this book could be deterrents. Now that we are confronted with a pandemic-gripped world, I have even wondered if a few of the ideas here might be useful springboards for those who are seizing the opportunity to re-design academic curriculum and delivery 'from the ground up'. But this book was originally meant simply as a sketch of my own thoughts, concerns, and biases about the ways in which we talk about music, and especially about ways in which we *could* talk about music, organized in a way that might stimulate reflection amongst like-minded participants.

The concept for this book was difficult in itself: it emerged out of preliminary work to prepare for dissemination of my own research about music (rhythm, analysis, multimedia, cognition, time, history). I realized, while trying to define both the scope of each topic and the order in which I should proceed, that I would need to qualify my perspectives on specific facets of music in order to make my conclusions intelligible. That is because my training, like that of many others, has been cross-disciplinary, and along paths that were not always well-charted, so that many terms and methodologies are still not well-established – especially trans-nationally. Yet I wanted to express my observations on these chosen topics in a way that specialists in other areas might decipher them, if interested.

As I struggled to present these perspectives in something other than a personal report, I began to imagine some frameworks that could be developed to help clarify any particular researcher's stance, so that such explanations could be attached to their profiles. In other words: as the cross-disciplinary crowd grows, the more useful it would be to have some means of identifying one's own and others' coordinates – a kind of scholar's GPS.

My first playful solutions as explained herein are meant merely as an impetus; as an artist recently working in more isolation than usual, I presume that others could refine these ideas if they seem to offer potential, or at least compare them with extant perspectives, or translate them into their own preferred idiom. But when I think how much these doubts and vague areas are slowing down my research, I cannot help but think that many others may be suffering exactly the same phenomena, if with different results. So a more organic solution seemed more likely to work in the short term: all it would take is for a few people to agree in principle – hence the idea of 'conversational musicologists'.

The majority of topics presented here are not novel, but some of them have developed within areas long considered 'peripheral' to the study of music, and as such, were typically ignored within core academic study in music. Although many of the topics are now benefitting from increasing attention from (small) groups of researchers around the world, they often stay within those communities for decades before being 'translated' into language that those in other communities can easily grasp. In particular, the findings are slow to permeate the foundations of training of any but those few, randomly-distributed institutions who have hired a bright and passionate researcher with both pedagogical and administrative skills, and given them the trust, latitude, and time to choose and refine course design and content.

As many of the general topics presented herein deal with very basic concepts, they tend to be avoided in discussion in academia where such generalities are considered unworthy, and one is supposed to keep complaints to oneself. However, everyone's individual stance on any of these topics probably influences their own interactions with music - although often unacknowledged except perhaps in casual conversation with friends. I propose that it is possible to build more environments and encourage strategies and behaviours to link between this conversational nature and the more typical 'scientific' model that has dominated so much of the Western academic stance, and which tries to strip away the emotions and personal tones of study to allow the "facts" to be viewed objectively. (Even though many of the recent trends focus more on the subjective experience of music, the language used to describe it is frequently too dense for the casual browser, and in some instances seems to try to apologize for its content.)

Music is often geared towards emotions; when it is more abstract it is often recognizable by the personal signature of the composer / performer(s). As our perception and reception of music is tied into very human and personal sensorial and cognitive systems, the scientific model in music – and now the newer philosophical models of expression - has often produced results that still fall quite short of explaining satisfactorily to the passionate listener, performer, or composer just why a certain piece is so entrancing and another one dull.

----- --- ----- --- -----

It will be quite apparent to some that my lifetime's explorations, as traceable here, were very typical of an artist: pursued in quite lateral fashion as first one model and then another attracted my interest. The organization of this book into sections and (mini-)chapters is simply one attempt to collect my thoughts into categories of relevant topics and strategies that could be folded into any general thinking about music. Of course, there are numerous possible groupings of the content, and doubtless some readers will notice gaping omissions (such as music therapy, opera, gender studies, and 'pop' music), but this particular configuration seems comprehensive enough for my own cross-disciplinary purposes, so I propose it as an illustration of the concept of possible groupings of concerns.

In particular, I wanted to throw into relief what I considered undue emphasis on a few of the topics to the detriment of others in my own training, which seems, sadly, still fairly typical of many North American curricula. Had my undergraduate years in the late 1970's included even one day's discussion on each of the topics in Chapters 7-35, for example, instead of three years' focus almost exclusively on a subsection of Chapter 9 (harmonic and formal analysis), I would have been much more adequately prepared for my subsequent explorations in composition, analysis, and teaching. Instead, I found myself wandering through uncharted territories, occasionally meeting other explorers (always stimulating) but largely unequipped to communicate my findings easily. Why? Because the areas that interest me – from unusual pitch structures and natural rhythms to electroacoustic music to perception / reception issues to the choosing of appropriate analytical methods – were so distant from standard theoretical discourse that it was not at all clear how they should be expressed.

I conceived of the idea of "conversational musicology" as a metaphor for a region that lies between 'chatting about music'

iv

and being 'professionally engaged in musicological research'. Those who would frequent this region are imagined as being primarily specialists (or specialists-in-training) - in one or two areas of any area of music or cognate disciplines - who would like to have an idea of what others are doing, and how their discoveries could be transferred to one's own explorations.

Music terms are used here generally in their broadest sense: thus the term "musicology" is treated to mean "the study of music". Likewise, "analysis" stretches from the initial mental comprehension of a musical or multimedia work to the traditional annotated graphs and score excerpts or academic discussions of socio-cultural reception. My particular view of these arrays are explained in subsequent chapters and in the appendices. Many other terms – pitch, rhythm, tuning, texture, etc. – are also discussed at length, as I argue that their meanings are not as universal as many seem to assume.

My recommendation for casual formats of dissemination – ranging from ones like this book to earnest conversations in the practice room - is based on a conviction that any serious quest for knowledge and understanding of musical traditions and individual masterpieces can benefit (at least occasionally) from contributions by non-musicologists. In other words, people who do not have the time, patience, dedication, language skills, opportunities, or confidence to present scholarly treatises at learned gatherings may possess insights that could escape a more pedantic approach - or at least communicate them more readily to others who don't have the patience or training for listening to a more lengthy discourse in impenetrable language. Also, it seems obvious that we each have preferences for specific types of voices for certain types of messages transmitted in particular environments. This can translate into the value of having something written or spoken in a style and pace that one enjoys, or at least is accessible, familiar, and non-stressful, while investigating a topic. It also fills the gap between a Facebook comment and a peer-reviewed journal article.

Increasingly, I am aware of a fairly marked difference between the way in which my peers and I were taught to think, research, and communicate and those of much younger participants. Not only the technological advantages and disadvantages but the overload of information often leads to a desperate attempt to keep abreast of current research. Thus, books that had a resonance for decades or centuries have become lost under a flurry of subsequent commentaries that often say close to the same thing, but less clearly. When a researcher does want to tap into older writings, the style and pace may seem opaque. For this reason also, these personal perspectives, if they multiply, might collectively provide useful indications of how older musicians think about music (and in general), and thereby illuminate the biases that are somewhat more hidden in extant academic communications - just as interviews with composers can often provide valuable insights that complement analyses of their works by professional theorists.

So, although this book was motivated initially simply by a need to explain my own background thinking – a summary of footnotes to future books on my worktable – I now intend it as encouragement to others in similar positions. If we wish to push the boundaries of what is 'acceptable' research discourse, and re-adjust priorities in music research, we could select some key terms and concepts that are tested for their intelligibility in multiple areas, and collectively create a network of explorers interested in comparing observations about the broader field of music and cognate areas. This would demand that the observations be made in a common or at least easily-decipherable language, and as a result we would naturally become more articulate and coherent in our conversations. In the spirit of artistic creation, rigorous research, building bridges, and providing food for thought, I am thus presenting a short survey of some topics I think merit reflection, with some of my own 'conversational asides' to illustrate.

Rosemary Mountain
October 2010 – May 2020
Canada / Europe

NOTES TO THE SECOND EDITION:

This edition was prepared in order to retain my original ideas about layout and style, fonts, margins, and other aspects that disappeared on conversion to the standard epub format. In particular I was aggrieved that the few diagrams and graphs and lists were not retained in a sensible way to be appreciated. Also, as footnotes were problematic, I incorporated some into the text, and have herein relegated them to their proper places.

As far as the verbal content goes, it remains essentially the same (with a few tweaks for clarity), as I have not seen more than a few attempts to remedy the general state of affairs, while the overwhelming proliferation of information and resulting drowning and difficulties in communication continue to accelerate. Although I could doubtless improve this book with a re-write, it seems less urgent than other projects.

I am happy to report that meanwhile my book summarizing my ideas about time (*A Musician's Guide to Time*) has now been published, and I was glad that I had written this one first, as it allowed me to avoid innumerable tangents in the second, as well as providing some explanation (and hopefully, justification) for its conversational style.

And now, having managed to complete these two books, I am spending more time on composing, which I consider more beneficial (for me and my listeners) than simply talking about music. However, I do wish that all who are interested in music could learn to be more comfortable with thinking about it and expressing their thoughts more clearly, if only to themselves and their closest friends - so if this book helps at all in creating such confidence, I will be pleased.

Rosemary Mountain
Halifax, Nova Scotia
October 2024

SECTION I

INTRODUCTION: MAPPING THE FIELD

This section identifies a problem in music research, and introduces the metaphors of "Conversational Musicology" and the "Conversational Musicologist"– terms used to describe a new (or revived) breed of articulate music explorers with characteristics such as the ability to convey ideas across disciplinary boundaries. I explain why such a breed would be useful, and speculate on what kind of training would be appropriate. Subsequently, I identify some of the main challenges of such a profile, such as sensitivity to different strategies and perspectives, and the courage to resist derision. Next, a wry glance is cast on the multitude of musicological sub-fields and their independence from each other. In conclusion, I mention a companion proposal for a 'tool kit' designed to highlight how different motivations for analysis will provoke different results, and what we might do to sort them out.

1

1. Conversational Musicology: what & why?

Musicology is, essentially, the study of music. Although this can take many forms, academia has tended to adapt the term to restrict it to the study of music by professional musicologists. The idea of 'conversational musicology' is to make this field a bit broader, more accessible to all musicians and any others who wish to participate. A related, if far-fetched, idea is that we might be able to acknowledge a variety of experts as being skilled (certified?!) Conversational Musicologists and hence well-adapted to offer guidance to any who wish to navigate the field or are wondering what paths to follow.

As with most professional fields, mainstream musicology tends to be transmitted among practitioners by standard forms, which emphasize the written score and the written word, preferably printed in reputable journals or with respected publishers, with specialized conferences for oral presentations and aural examples - where normally the best presentations will be transferred to written formats, although sometimes with graphics and even sonic footnotes.

Music is, however, very much an aural art. Many people who participate in creating or appreciating the art – for example composers, performers, film-makers, passionate listeners, and even some of the 'fringe' musicologists – have insights that are not always easily expressed in the written format of disciplined prose. Even among scholarly musicians, useful perspectives shared in one 'camp' or sub-discipline are often slow to be communicated, recognized, and appreciated in other camps. The current book argues that we would benefit from a wider realm of discourse – wider in the sense not only of the subject matter but also the perspectives and the means of expressing them.

The metaphor of "conversational musicology" is

designed to incorporate the idea of a bridge between the poetry of musical art and the prose of scholarly criticism. The concept works best when treated playfully, but is designed at one level to invoke the popular method for language acquisition: lessons on pronunciation, basic vocabulary, cursory knowledge of syntax, some stock idiomatic phrases, and a few hints about the peculiarities of the specific culture. The aim of such language-learning techniques is to provide guidance to those who wish to jump into a foreign culture and start navigating in it, sharing information and ideas with its people, without having to devote preliminary years of study to the language structures. In such an analogy, "conversational musicology" extends the idea of a 'basic vocabulary' to include all kinds of terminology, concepts and repertoire; acknowledges that each 'camp' (historian, theorist, composer, performer, listener, sound engineer, critic, teacher) has its own range of strategies and worldviews; and suggests that these meanings are further nuanced by the genre or type under discussion (electroacoustics, blues, serial music, Brahms...). Syntax can be understood as the methodologies used (written analyses, detailed observations) in conjunction with the style and context of the dialogue (formal high-brow academic tone versus an online forum or a discussion during rehearsal). The 'stock idiomatic phrases' could be interpreted as the most quoted bibliography - and biases - of each camp, although it might be amusing to indulge a more literal interpretation.

An associated idea is to stake out a territory, most likely in the form of a network of pathways which is at times adjacent to those of musicological research, but not demanding the same degree of formality or professional dedication. This would become the realm of Conversational Musicology and would, like all the other areas, have its own perspectives and strategies. But rather

3

than always looking directly at music and musicians, the conversational musicologists would also be looking at / chatting with all the others who are involved with music, to see what might be discovered. As the accepted means of transmitting observations in this realm would be more in the conversational nature, the languages (verbal or non-verbal) used for expression would be designed to ease cross-disciplinary discourse. Eventually, perhaps, it would become standard practice for departments to have Conversational Musicology seminars, and for all kinds of research teams to include at least one Conversational Musicologist to help ensure that relevant research was identified and 'translated' into more appropriate language and means for consumption by others in cognate areas. It is not conceived of as being a 'popularist' in the sense of providing complex ideas to people completely out of the field, where such results are usually too simplistic for any expert, but rather a way of reinstating communication among musicians (and other interested explorers) of various specializations.

A new breed of semi-academics has emerged in recent decades whose practice is often known as 'artist-as-research' or 'practice-as-research'. They are known in Quebec, and much of Canada, and some other parts of the world, as "researcher-creators". The idea is that rather than conducting research in a traditional way through the study of existing data, one uses a combination of critical analysis (usually verbally expressed) and artistic forms (e.g. using non-verbal language). In one way, my concept of Conversational Musicology is to the traditional musicologist as the researcher-creator is to the (non-practice-based) researcher or the (inarticulate) artist.

THE PROBLEM: INFORMATION OVERLOAD AND OTHER FACTORS

There is a major problem in music research these days, but although it is quite easy to explain, it seems rarely acknowledged – probably because (a) the causes are linked to the integral part of our recent history; (b) it could be a source of embarrassment; and (c) solutions seem elusive.

The main cause is simply the proliferation, in the past century, of music, musicians, and music research. The 20th-century explosion of diverse musical styles and genres, and our increasing exposure to the art of multiple cultures and eras, eventually triggered a corresponding diversity of analytical approaches within musicological communities. The sheer number of participants also grew exponentially. Music now has so many acknowledged facets, and participants, that conversations about music in any but the most formal situations – for example a specialized conference - involve different perspectives and different 'core repertoire'. Researchers and non-researchers cluster into groups of 'like-minded' people who meet to discuss a shared passion. Subsequently, these groups often develop their own strategies for study and discussion, complete with specialized terminology and shared jokes: hardly any cause for complaint.

But the result is that we now have too much information to handle, and the field is too vast for coherence. Research is disseminated in different formats & languages – literally and figuratively – and therefore it is difficult to navigate and digest. (There are other factors involved too that will be discussed further on.) As a result, the flow of information between different sub-fields has become more stagnant, with highly-qualified experts from different areas often unable to enter into fruitful discussions because their paths have been so divergent that they don't have enough in

5

common – methodologies, repertoire, terminology – to share observations.

The problem is exacerbated by several factors:

- a proliferation of sub-disciplines, each with its own terminology and approaches, even though many cover similar territories;

- overwhelming numbers of writings being disseminated and composers and artistic works being discovered, both contemporary and historical, as the traditionally narrow post-Renaissance Western European focus becomes at last (thankfully) replaced with a wider window;

- ease of access to information, which serves to emphasize the number of extant books, articles, and music;

- a proliferation of publishers and means of dissemination which thwarts a traditional function of publisher as filterer and pronouncer of quality (actually, articulate or powerful proponents of their own aesthetics & values); and

- a tendency shared by many people who want to belong to a club and develop a kind of code and behaviour that allows efficient (or at least enjoyable) internal communication, and effective exclusion of annoying bystanders.

For those safely ensconced in one sub-field, even this state of affairs may not appear to be a problem. But for many of us whose research is cross-disciplinary, or at least straddling two or more 'camps', the current situation needs improving. One assumes that it would be possible to create more favourable conditions for anticipating a diversity of perspectives, and refine some strategies for cross-disciplinary discourse. Until we have a more sophisticated protocol for discussion, I propose that the extension of the concept of conversation into "conversational musicology" could encourage people to express ideas even when they are outside their own area of expertise, and even if the ideas themselves are nebulous, as long as that is acknowledged. Local chapters could organize topics for their monthly meetings over tapas, for example. As a bonus, young researchers trying to find a suitable topic for a dissertation might discover some ideas in need of investigation, or at least find some useful tools and frameworks for researching their own field.

A first challenge, but one that seems surmountable, would be to map out all the different areas of musical interest – from film music to music therapy – in such a way that (potential) overlaps, common interests, shared methodologies, and resources are more easily demonstrated. If we extend the metaphor of the map to the closely-related guidebook, we could incorporate a description of the various characteristics of each field and sub-field. This way, an interested explorer can navigate more efficiently to the most appropriate means and resources for studying a specific aspect or issue involving music.

In the very large field of music analysis, even the process of identifying and cataloguing the diversity of approaches would be quite helpful.[1] Chapter 6 of this book describes one sketch (*"Tool Kit for Music Analysis"*) that involves a database, checklists, and a short guide. That proposal is based on a conviction that there are factors in analysis that seem to sit outside the analysis itself but which affect the results and could well be acknowledged. The *Tool Kit* is the kind of project that would benefit from numerous participants, but can also be refined and used by a single researcher, because it is concerned with discovering how best to study a musical work - or any artwork created with sonic elements incorporated into the design.

---

1. However, caveats to such an approach are described later in Ch. 33.

On a larger scale, however, when we are looking for a guide to subfields and their accompanying research activities, the idea of a mega-database becomes quite inadequate for spotting intersections and shared or conflicting concerns and terminologies. For one thing, it would be unrealistic to imagine that enough people could contribute to ensure a sufficiently comprehensive and constantly-updated guide with hyperlinks between all intersecting areas. In addition, not all the relevant information would be appropriately classified under the same template. More importantly, not everyone concerned would want to interact with this kind of information via an internet-based wiki or other wordy table format: the information presented in such forms is usually suited to more static things, and not always linked to knowledge in a straightforward way.[2] And crucially, it would be unrealistic to imagine that all aspects of music research or acknowledgement of its character (and that of its proponents) would fit comfortably in the rational, fixed universe of a database.

If we substitute humans for a database, however, we might be able to solve many of the problems. For example, we could imagine a special breed of music researcher-guide-translator who would be qualified to guide interested persons through the complex jungle of talk, research, and interpretation relating to music. If there were a substantial number of acknowledged experts who are aware of diverse areas within the current state of research, they could be well-qualified to foster links between different individuals, groups, and communities. Assuming that such a genre would take a decade to define and a further half-century to become recognized as a viable 'career path', I am proposing

---

2. In fact, many of the potential participants are those who intuitively or consciously try to reduce the amount of time spent in front of a computer screen – while some of us suspect that no robust solution should depend exclusively on the availability of internet &/ or electricity.

that some of us who enjoy thinking about many different facets of music and research simply pronounce ourselves "proto-Conversational Musicologists" while standards for certification are established. In the meantime, perhaps some Conversational Musicologist Clubs could self-form in different regions, where nomadic visitors could drop in to find out about local researchers and their ideas. This also points out that Conversational Musicologists work best when in collaboration: as no one will ever be able to be current in all areas of research even with the field of music, it becomes essential to find a few fellow researchers with whom one can productively share ideas - in person when possible.

The broader approach of Conversational Musicology, on the other hand, is more accessible to anyone. In this scenario, each informally self-labelled conversational musicologist would be familiar at ease in several different areas of music, and familiar with music-related research and/or practitioners. Being receptive to ideas about music from a greater variety of sources involves "developing an ear" for the "dialects" of other specialists, and having a more comprehensive knowledge of the history and culture of at least some. Only some people would have the personality to be interested (unless this evolved into a well-paying profession): a blend of diplomacy, curiosity of what others are doing and listening to, and a natural expressivity to permit communicating even without a well-established formal language in common. Thus they would be well-qualified to serve as 'translators' from the jargon and perspective of one sub-field to another – able to warn the novice about inherent biases in the particular trade, recommend protocol, etc. In the function of 'travel guides', they could inform interested explorers about the particular habits and current trends of the specialists in various given fields. They could meet periodically with spokespeople from each area who enjoy explaining their research topics, events, strategies, and quandaries to a sympathetic colleague. Eventually, when there are enough people flourishing at such tasks, a profile of the ideal articulate, multi-lingual diplomat / travel guide would emerge, allowing such functions to be acknowledged as potentially comparable to specialists in terms of quality and integrity.

Conversations, unlike published journal articles, are not in as much need of carefully-explained conclusions; they are a more typical context for expressing hunches. In the early days of the internet, this naturally led to 'chat rooms' and focus groups in many of the music research sub-fields. However, it becomes impractical to have such dedicated forums that would work across disciplines – and such forums usually limit the participants to the more serious professional researchers (by context and style if nothing else), filtered by those not allergic to internet / screen dependency, rather than those whose focus tends more to the practical (such as performers and composers). The idea behind the *Conversational Musicology* proposal is that by announcing our intentions through such a label, we could enrich the discourse. In addition, by giving some serious thought to the matter, we can presumably improve the signal-to-noise ratio that usually characterizes casual conversations.

The incorporation of self-referential experience into conversations, and personal-style writing within academic discourse, are anathema to many rational-minded people. But it can be helpful, with some likeness to the ways in which metaphors are helpful, in that the personal tone of conversations can permit the listeners to adjust their filters so that they understand the person speaking. (An initially startling but highly effective example was provided by Katherine Norman - and her students - in her book

Sounding Art.) Much of what makes up our preferences for musical and analytical approaches is linked with our own cultural and musical upbringing and learning environments – and those are often revealed in the means of expression, but less often acknowledged in rational contexts. In the old days, it was simple: one talked with one's society peers – collectively, *us*, who did things in the most reasonable way, and then there were *others*, who did things differently and from whom one would not expect to learn, nor expect to be understood. Even though many people in our 'post-colonial' Western world will imagine that they have learned to be tolerant of other races and cultures, they may not extend this to a more conceptual level of practitioners in a cognate area. As a result, the multiple filters of participants in music discourse can produce quite distorted images. This is why it might be useful to try identifying the main areas and types of filters that music researchers are likely to apply, so that the interested researcher could use this as a kind of 'checklist'.

As mentioned above, the topics discussed herein - ranging from aesthetics and acoustic ecology to cognitive sciences and multimedia analysis – are frequently treated as 'peripheral' to a professional Western music education and/or 'irrelevant' to a particular focus. As such, they have often suffered from a lack of critical attention, especially in academic contexts. Hence, a researcher's individual stance on any of these topics may be influential in their own interactions with music, but unacknowledged. My proposed first step is that by constructing simple lists of potentially relevant topics and exposing them to critical scrutiny (individually or collectively), aspiring Conversational Musicologists could survey any chosen topic through a variety of lenses before choosing the most appropriate one to pursue. Conversely, if working as a 'translator' to explain research in one field to someone in another, one could more quickly recognize the respective emphases. For instance, at a very basic level: when dealing in artistic collaboration, it becomes essential to clarify the different usages of words like 'texture' and 'gesture' that may have clear but often incompatible meanings in dance, visual arts, music, and architecture.[3] And if one or more of the collaborators is not an artist, it may become necessary – if possible – to explain the artists' dependency on periods of lateral thinking and impromptu changes.

As university groups brainstorm to re-think curricula, it might also be worth assuming, for example, that if one allots only four semesters for music theory basics, it might be wise to re-structure it from the ground up, rather than trying to squeeze increasing amounts of material into the same time slot. As I imagine it (and practiced it, with good results), the students should be exposed to examples of the widest range of music possible and the widest range of analytical perspectives, and given some protective gear and some concise guides of how to choose the best perspective(s), the best tools, and the best instructions or models of how to apply them.

Most of the issues addressed here, from aesthetics and pedagogy to musical organization and analytical approaches, might be effectively introduced conceptually into a foundation course to help frame all subsequent teaching and research avenues. This would be compatible with a review of the skills required for all the opportunities that exist in the music world, from festival promoter to sound engineer to music psychology to therapy. Likewise,

---

3. A slowly-developing partner project to this book involves the assembly of auditory & multimedia examples along with very short texts to explain terms and concepts of such things as pitch, gesture, spectromorphology, and consonance so that anyone interested - whether musicians or other artists or researchers - can begin to understand what is meant, without being obliged to take a course or two. See Appendix D.

it would be useful to sketch out the extent of traditional and current research in all of the various areas, so that students would have some notion of the vastness of the field, the number of ways in which it can be studied, and the immense potential for making connections in new ways.[4] Subsequently, Western concepts of tonal music, for example, would be grasped as just one popular way of segmenting and prioritizing the various components of musical experience - which many Western composers abandoned with excellent results in the 20th century. The equal-tempered scale would similarly be presented as just one subset of temperament and pitch schema, while pitch and instrumentation could be better understood as a traditional (but not typically 20th century) Western way of conceptualizing timbre and frequency.

---

4. Of course, this would be further enhanced by a general non-music elective formulated to do the same at a broader level - indicating for example all the major disciplines and their standard intersections, and how they match the increasingly erratic distribution of courses into particular departments and faculties.

2. Terrors of interdisciplinarity (*or:* Jack-of-all-trades)

Musical sub-disciplines have become so independent from each other that moving from one to another can appear cross-disciplinary. There are several problems that hamper communication between them, but most of them seem to arise from the following (intertwined) points:

TRADITION: Scholarly tradition encourages lively conversation between 'peers' in a field, but seems to discourage 'loose talk' between musicologists and others whose expertise is not so clearly defined. This was probably fueled by the shift in the humanities in the early 20th century to emulate the scientific communities' regard for 'rigorous objectivity'.[5]

BEHAVIOUR: Musicologists are encouraged to be scholarly, organized, rational, etc. whereas composers and performers benefit greatly from entertaining instinct, irrationality, feeling, expression, the playful, etc. Therefore, the two (or more) 'types' regard each other with suspicion [see also Hostile Attitudes and Other Obstacles, below].

INFORMATION OVERLOAD: As specialist fields emerge and develop, they are accompanied by a proliferation of terminologies, books, conferences, common reference material, etc., that overwhelm the researcher until time runs out and communication between specialists and non-specialist becomes scarce.

LANGUAGE & TERMINOLOGIES: Invented and borrowed terms, visual annotations, analogies, and devices used to

---

5. As usual when one group copies from another, the solutions may also lag behind: the impossibility of subtracting the observer from the observation has been recognized long since in science – along with other useful aspects like fuzzy logic, chaos theory, and the uncertainty principle – but is still hard to dislodge from some of the scholarly branches of humanities.

describe audio and other invisible temporal aspects are often chosen or adopted without sufficient care to their other attributes, and subsequently hinder discourse. There is also the bias of language style, which may be comprehensible across disciplines but not across genres or age groups, let alone across linguistic divides.

TRAINING: As with many fields, music and sound are incorporated into a variety of areas and contexts: audio engineering schools, conservatories, film music workshops, university degree programmes. Usually, those designing the curricula are not professionally-trained curriculum designers, nor do they have the freedom to create courses that are shorter, longer, or in different formats than the standard.

ENVIRONMENT: Pressures of the workplace (committee meetings rather than music symposia, permanent connection to the rest of the world, sheer noise) lead to insufficient time to think and articulate clearly. This is compounded by institutional, peer, or career pressure to publish prematurely or in an inappropriate format. How many institutions value the stimulating colleague who helps promote intellectual reflection in the faculty lounge?

DIFFERING WORLD-VIEWS: A further impediment to communication is when we encounter a clash of 'world-views': these range from views of historical linearity to occupational priorities and personalities.

HOSTILE ATTITUDES: Such attitudes, springing from a myriad of motivations and triggered even by dress or gender, can be found in young undergraduates and senior scholars alike, and can easily hinder a free exchange of ideas.

It seems that several of these factors would be mitigated if there were more open acknowledgement and discussion of them. However, it is clear that most of them do not qualify directly as topics for musicology – hence this proposal that we define a new subfield where such topics *are* intertwined into discussion of music and sound.

OTHER OBSTACLES: Additional factors that are even more difficult to expose to scrutiny include the following common deficiencies in the available specialist resources (including teachers, colleagues, collaborators, etc.):

- lack of exposure to academic discussion outside one's own specializations;

- lack of awareness of the appropriation and specialized usage of words in one's own subfield, or of one's own use of uncommon words (typical in music, where we routinely re-define words [dynamics, articulation, temperament, horizontal / vertical, up/down], often taking them out of three-dimensional contexts, and frequently use other less-known ones borrowed from other languages [like timbre, *legato*, and *pianissimo*]);

- reliance on published work of contemporaries or predecessors to articulate pivotal concepts, rather than attempting to internalize and express in one's own words – the tendency to parrot rather than synthesize;

- pressure to be 'contemporary' and to disdain relevant contributions from earlier decades / centuries – many of which are in fact more understandable to a wider audience, as they may predate specialist terminologies;

- a sense of unease at being unable to communicate with a non-specialist - i.e. explaining essential principles or ideas without recourse to specific books, concepts, repertoire, or terminology.

JACK-OF-ALL-TRADES: The net result of all this is often one of insecurity, accentuated by derision towards the explorer who wanders into a different sub-field: the 'jack-of-all-trades' taunt. "Jack-of-all-trades" in itself seems not a bad moniker, but is invariably linked, if unspoken, with the derisive "and master of none". (On the other hand, the word 'polymath' seems to be attributed as a very high honour reserved for a very special few. Why do we not acknowledge "budding polymaths" – or even try to grow them?) The thrill of chatting with a specialist in any field of interest can be replaced by embarrassment at the inevitable "You've never read Dr. X?" The more inexperienced run back to their libraries, and try to read the author in question. But typically, that book assumes an intimate knowledge of at least a dozen more books, each of which assumes an intimate knowledge of at least a dozen more books, and so on.... As all interdisciplinary researchers have noticed, there are just too many books to read, even disregarding all but the most cogent, concise, articulate, and relevant to our study - and how would we know which those are? Information overload again.

Of course, encouraging a general interest in all kinds of things may result initially in a scant knowledge of all subjects – this is the main fear and it is not unreasonable. But presumably, when we start with a general exposure to context, and exercise more involvement in the choice of subject, it becomes helpful for subsequent intensive training in the intellectual and emotional realm of music. In other words, finding the path to town is easier when one has stood on the hilltop to survey the landscape and viewed the possibilities.

In the old days, these issues were not so pronounced. In mainstream Western European culture of the 19th and early 20th centuries at least, conservatories were places for training the specialist performer: instrumentalists and singers, dancers, actors. The artists – composers, playwrights, choreographers, painters – came generally from upper-class families where they were given a very broad education and socialized with people from many different areas. Therefore, their ideas were populated from a vast array of disciplines – poetry, natural science, philosophy, mythology.... In the 20th century, with a new 'democratic' order, composition and other creative arts were added to the conservatory rostrum – but never fit quite as well, as the broad base was never attended to.[6] Subsequently, in North American music education at least, most of the training has migrated to universities, where musicology fits quite comfortably, but composition and performance less so – meaning that they are at a disadvantage to make themselves understood to their more academic colleagues. Despite the grouping together of performers, composers, and musicologists (and sometimes artists from other disciplines) within single institutions, specialists in musicology are often ill-prepared for confrontation with the artists for whom they are sometimes thought to advocate: artists in particular are likely to "take poetic license" or to imbue their arguments with passion, sometimes just for the sheer effect on their audience.

Meanwhile, increasing numbers of public elementary and high schools (and occasionally universities) are contributing to the difficulty by striking music and art off the curriculum altogether – as well as some basic written communication skills.[7] As a result, both the centrality of non-verbal communication and its various forms and languages become increasingly remote from non-specialists.

Similarly, there are numerous scholars who have a tendency to scoff at new and different ways of looking at things, new hypotheses, new hunches. History abounds with examples of these: the apparently ludicrous idea that the earth revolves around the sun, or that the different continents are attached to shifting tectonic plates. Slonimsky's *Lexicon of Musical Invective* provides some

6. Thanks to Sandeep Bhagwati for reminding me of this factor.

7. Handwriting, spelling, and grammar, for example.

18

nice illustrations from the music criticism world. As those artistically inclined already know, the simple mental exercise of assuming momentarily that any given hunch might be true can be a healthy and rather stimulating activity. On the other hand, the need for skepticism is essential at some level, so those who seem to entertain every hunch they encounter will likely become ostracized. Therefore, if the hunch turns out not to make sense (which is of course quite typical), those who thought it interesting will more likely be deprived of the arguments that prove it wrong. Many hunches do however have a grain of interest, if not truth, and can open the discourse to unexpected and beneficial perspectives.

The impact of the 'enlarged' dimensions of the field of musicology may be profound for many scholars, simply in terms of vastness: provoking a 'scholarly agoraphobia'. In order to have an understanding of the field in general, it is necessary to understand a bit of all the component areas, yet that tends to preclude the work necessary to becoming a specialist – including the habits and research strategies of developing deep understanding. Without being a specialist, one can hardly appreciate the nuances of each component, or distinguish between good and poor scholarship, or even have the necessary basics to carry on a good conversation with colleagues in a sub-area. Certainly, the chances are rare of making any significant contribution to any one field without devoting years of study to it. Conferences of large groups like the *International Musicological Society* do collectively display an amazing amount of research – but many graduate students and junior faculty members must find that their initial delight in being selected to present a paper and in obtaining the necessary funding to attend becomes quickly overwhelmed by the hundreds of delegates and parallel sessions confronting them. Choosing whom to talk with and listen to is a task that requires not only hours of specific preparation, but preferably years of browsing a wider variety of music journals and conference proceedings than one's local library carries, in addition to studying some corpus of music in depth.

As a result, far too many people - including those with advanced degrees in music - seem unaware of the vast array of valid and interesting ways to reflect on, think about, and study music. Even worse, those who *are* aware of the multitude of approaches rarely know where to begin or how to find out what might reward further study. The idea of this book is to stimulate some discussion about how to navigate the variety and how to choose which approach might be the most rewarding for the intended purpose.

3. Historical connections & non-linear views
(*or:* Playing Follow-the-Dots)

One further item is an obstacle only if one does not recognize its potential as a game: linear *vs.* non-linear views of history. An extremely popular view of music history (in Western academic contexts at least) is intertwined with the parallel and even more pervasive view of Western European history. That is one which reconstructs the past in view of our preferred view of the present, and explains the move from the earlier stage to the later as at least somewhat inevitable, and usually as a more or less constant improvement. This view is so central to much of Western society that it is often difficult to examine critically. The element of change, which is more visible to an historian of recent times, is normally considered to be indicative of a state of growth – or more recently, a state of decline - because most people, it seems, would prefer to imagine a non-chaotic world.

The linearity of this view of history and time has an intrinsic problem of being related, normally, by the conqueror, and therefore emphasizing certain aspects while ignoring, or erasing, the more objectionable moments such as the virtues of the culture of the conquered. In today's world, other views are more frequently presented, but usually with equivalent filters and biases. However, a more subtle casualty of the linear view is the range of contrasting cyclic models of time that imply recurring growth and decay, as in 'the rise and fall of civilizations'. Although that metaphor may be familiar to many, there is still a tendency to see primarily one's own surroundings, or 'civilization', in a linear sense. Even the metaphor of 'globalization' argues that it is more useful, or important, to see us all as one group, with a common fate – rather than appreciating the plurality of multiple ebbs and flows. This globalization view of humanity is easily promoted through both internet and social media, as well as a sense of all of us being susceptible to the actions or events elsewhere, from pollution to climate change to waves of mass migration or viruses. Current political conditions, fuelled by deliberate media policies and numerous artistic and commercial portrayals of "Dystopia", have popularized the concept of a downward slide without much anticipation of a future growth. However, these views often obscure the fact that humans used to have quite different histories and were largely ignorant of others. (A simple example is that of the still-popular view that "the Dark Ages' was a universal stage of history, rather than a state restricted to north & central Europe – as can be shown quite strikingly by a cursory study of cultural life in the Iberian peninsula between CE 8th to 16th centuries.)

Regardless of these trends, an increasing number of scholars in various fields are speculating on more complex models of history, culture, and time, in which the concept of a single 'culture' or 'civilization' is of limited usefulness. With the increased attention to demographics in today's business world, we can invent multiple ways to link contemporary and past things, whether events, styles, trends, people, etc. Music is equally viable to view in a number of ways. Compositional concepts and techniques that seem to have emerged 'out of nowhere' can be traced, in retrospect and through clever (and at times, spurious) sleuthing, to contributing factors – even if they are only connected conceptually, in retrospect. Distinct compositional styles of the 20th century can be shown to coexist even within the population segments previously considered to belong to a 'homogenous' culture. Composers in one 'school' learn from each other's experiments while completely ignoring those in another. Conversely, increasing numbers of musicians are combining elements of music that previously belonged to distinct cultures. Cross-cultural comparisons are used to develop new perspectives and frameworks for comprehension. Likewise, cross-disciplinary studies are proliferating, and concepts and strategies lent, borrowed, and fused. New technologies add research tools, strategies, and models - as well as certain frustrations and restrictions.

What is the impact of all of this on analysis? It makes for endless ways to 'connect the dots'. One can compare music on the basis of instrumentation or intent; composer's gender, or nationality, or skill; performance, venue, audience; its appropriation in advertising or propaganda; etc. One can choose to 'focus on the music itself' - but what does this mean? The score, the performance, its reception?

Not all contemporary composers are influenced by the same list of predecessors. In this age of thousands of contemporary composers, none of us will have an intimate acquaintance with all the ones we are "meant" to know. In addition, as composition students seem naturally rebellious, we often reject works much more strongly than our classmates do. This is actually a very efficient strategy: we may be rejecting on the basis of elements that we could not precisely articulate, but we arrive at defining our own preferred aesthetic 'slate' more quickly. Conversely, we may 'fall in love' with a particular piece – often based on a particular passage or formal consideration – and play it over many more times than our peers would think 'necessary'. Unfortunately, we do not always acknowledge what our influences are (at least when young), so the strategy of simply asking a composer about his or her influences does not always guarantee an accurate answer – but it is certainly a good start. It is rather surprising to me that music students are so seldom encouraged to reflect on what music they like and what music they don't.[8]

---

8. See Ch. 26 on Aesthetics for more discussion.

A further rather interesting, if under-employed, benefit of this view of history is that it allows the composer to pick her own 'evolution' in terms of the lineage she is most interested in being a part of.[9] In such a case, the urgency to keep up with latest trends disappears – especially if one feels that certain experiments a century or two ago never received the attention they merited (usually because someone or something more dramatic arrived on the scene) and are worthy of continued development. The only challenge with this is developing higher-quality marketing tools – or at least common terminologies – which will allow those who share aesthetic tastes and artistic interests to discover new participants. Roving conversational musicologists could help....

---

9. See Ch. 6 for more on lineage.

4. Musicologists – who and why? (or: Mapping the fields of analysis & musicology)

Musicology can sound like forbidden territory to non-musicologists: a field that is populated only by the most academic of academics. The idea of "Conversational Musicology" is to make this territory slightly less forbidding, by sculpting and maintaining paths that wander close by the musicologists' various sub-fields (maintaining a discreet distance, of course). This path would be open to everyone, and frequented by certified Conversational Musicologists, who would be available as guides and translators for the various areas.

Not so many decades ago, the field of musicology was viewed by many of the rest of us in its narrowest sense of historical musicology, and conjured up a vision of the most conservatively-dressed, often male, member of the music faculty who was very knowledgeable about a specific composer and period of history (usually, it seemed, 18th- or 19th-century German or Austrian, or possibly Italian, if operatic), and thus not only a formidable scholar, but also one rather distant from contemporary music-making. Fortunately, some very strong proponents of other approaches to musicology have successfully broken that image. Nonetheless, some of those involved with music who are *not* musicologists have difficulty understanding why we need musicologists at all. On the other hand, talking about music if one is not a musicologist can seem almost illegal, at least in academic circles.

The dominance of 18th- and 19th-century European classical score-based analysis, along with certain traditions of scholarship, began to alienate some music researchers in the 20th century who then organically formed different groups with their own approaches: conferences, journals, terminologies. Nowadays, we have myriads of examples of how to study music - but not enough generalists (or what I like to label "translators") to explain what everyone is talking about, and to spot duplications, reinforcements, opposing evidence, etc.

For example, the different groups have coalesced for a variety of reasons, including apparently irrelevant ones like geographical proximity, writing style, or personality. All it takes is eight or ten motivated researchers in one city, or even within one pan-European university network, to instigate a 'research cluster', complete with funding, which will then organize symposia. Eventually, if interesting and/or well-funded and/or populated by administratively-adept members, the group can become a more formal organization, and even define a sub-field in music research. Therefore, group boundaries overlap, intersect, contradict, and betray their own perspectives by their own identifications. Trying to organize the various types of musicologists and "sister disciplines" by proximity of strategy or focus can be a useful exercise: like a game, the pieces can be re-arranged according to different sorting criteria, and the attempt to find similarities can prompt deeper reflection: see *Figure 1* for a possible arrangement.

Considerable overlap exists between the three most common divisions: theory, musicology, and analysis. To make matters more complicated, there seems to be a difference between music theory, as an area of study, and the music theorist as a professional specialist; there are also different usages of these terms between countries. These differences are acute to some of the practitioners, but often quite unrecognized by those just slightly distant from the specialist camps – such as students, and performers.

MUSIC THEORY: In most North American university music programmes, at least, "theory" is the branch of the

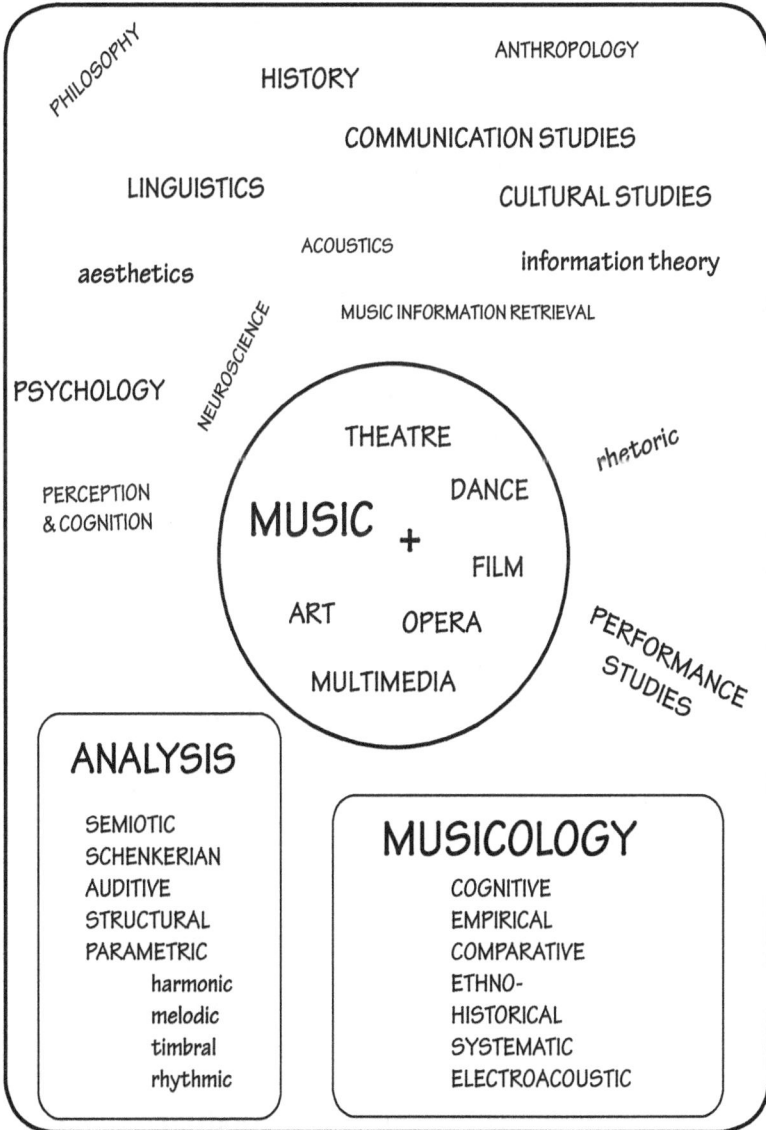

FIGURE 1: Musicology-& some cognate disciplines & sub-disciplines

programme that deals with the terminologies, structures, forms, and other basic aspects of music - based generally on explanations of historical usage, perusal of notated scores, and exercises in analyzing scores of (mainly 18th and 19th-century) compositions according to harmonic aspects and formal structures as they compare to "models" (of, for example, sonata-allegro form). "Analysis" is often the title of one to four semesters' worth of courses within the undergraduate "theory" stream; "theory" often refers to the rudiments and is replete with artificial examples while "analysis" implies a more engaged application of the 'rules' to identify elements and structures of real compositions, usually drawn from a central corpus that is rarely renewed. At a graduate level, on the other hand, a student working in "theory" is usually working on new ways of examining these elements. Therefore, it seems that "theory" applies to the most general and basic, whereas "theorist" is the rarest breed of inventor or identifier of rules that could be or have been used for musical organization.

MUSICOLOGY is a field whose definitions are fuzzy, and depend to some extent on regional shading. Ostensibly, a musicologist is one who studies music. Over the past century, there has been a proliferation of sub-fields of musicology to include historical, empirical, systematic, cognitive, cooperative, ethno-, electroacoustic, etc. (These various sub-fields are described further in Appendices A & B.) There are many regional, national, and international societies, journals, websites, research centres, etc. dealing with each of these areas; a few (notably the *International Musicological Society*) embrace all sub-fields although one will rarely find someone who has a good grasp of all of them even in general terms.

ANALYSIS: As in other disciplines, the term implies a detailed examination of a thing in an attempt to understand its structure. There are sub-fields of music study that are more often described not as types of musicology but rather as types of analysis. *Figure 2* provides one way of summarizing these different types. Although this seems to me a viable summary, its reflection in academia is quite skewed: the emphasis in most Western undergraduate music programmes until very recently was not only restricted to parametric analysis, but usually specifically on harmonic and formal analysis, with scant regard for timbre, texture, and intonation and little emphasis on rhythmic organization. In addition, music which was presented in different ways - such as electronically, or as part of a multi-media installation - are often completely ignored as being too far away from the main corpus.[10]

As a result, many of the innovative works of the 20th century were marginalized in the musicological field as their attributes are inadequately demonstrated by these means - whether they were score-less ephemeral 'happenings', or focussed on timbral elements, non-harmonic structures, and/or non-standard temperament for which traditional notation is inadequate. To put it another way: if one imagined all the analysts as being in one building, and each floor of the building devoted to one of the five major groups listed here, and each room on the Parametric Analysis floor devoted to one of the eight subcategories, etc., then a visitor would notice that the majority of the participants were in the same corner of the same room. Nowadays, more of the rooms are populated, but most remain in one spot, and there are still very few in the 'Associative / Mood / Imagery' room, for example, despite the enormous relevance for analyzing music composed specifically for film, dance, and installations. On the other hand, a high proportion of those in the 'timbre' and 'gesture' rooms seem to be involved in electroacoustics, where both pitch and notation are often absent and thus other elements have needed further

---

10. Additionally, it led to studying works like Stravinsky's *Rite of Spring* without mentioning the accompanying stomps of feet.

PARAMETRIC ANALYSIS

- PITCH - modality, tuning, harmony

- RHYTHM - durational patterns, phrase structure

- DYNAMICS – both absolute and relative loudness of individual parts and their combination

- TIMBRE - instrumentation, articulation, spectromorphology (includes dynamics at some level)

- PITCH+RHYTHM (+ DYNAMICS) - melody, harmony, motive

- FORM / STRUCTURE

- TEXTURE (19th & 20th c meanings [see Ch. 13])

- GESTURE

SEMIOTIC ANALYSIS

STYLISTIC / CONTEXTUAL ANALYSIS

SOCIO-POLITICAL ANALYSIS (HISTORICAL/CULTURAL)

ASSOCIATIVE / MOOD / IMAGERY

FIGURE 2. Various types of analytical approaches

attention.[11]

The specific types and categories could be presented in different configurations, but the analogy remains. Each approach has merits that make it appropriate for a particular type of study. For example: improvisation is central to some music (such as free jazz), but rather insignificant for others - such as Boulez's *Structures* (although ironically the results may seem similar). Therefore, although an historical approach could work well for either type by identifying contemporary trends that created a fertile context for their emergence, a parametric approach might be more suitable for the Boulez and a performance / aural approach more suitable for the free jazz. On the other hand, *Structures* makes an ideal example for an introduction to music perception, as human perceptual tendencies such as registral and temporal proximity (see Ch. 23) can give a very different picture of links between notes than those suggested by the conventions of serialism.

On another level, the composer may have incorporated a kind of improvisation into the compositional process, which might be a useful aspect to study in some circumstances, though difficult to demonstrate without some kind of corroboration from the composer him/ herself. Even such corroboration is risky, as composers are not always the most objective reporters of their own *modi operandi*; many contemporary composers in the later 20th century were reluctant to admit that personal aesthetics and intuition played a vital role in their creative work, and were likely to agree with a sympathetic critic who invented more rational motivations for them.

A different facet of this issue of perspective / skew is in the disappearance of cues from the original context. One example is the use of rhetorical devices, transferred from

---

11. See Chs. 9 and 10.

oration practice to music by composers of the Baroque period in particular. The art of rhetoric was once a part of the standard classical education, and it was natural that its expression in music became a deliberate art. Intervening fashion, however, has obscured the oral tradition of the community, and rhetoric is generally a foreign subject to a Western-centred music education. It therefore seems important, if studying works where such devices existed, that the analyst should at least be aware of the potential influence of such factors and understand that resources exist to explain them in more detail.

Perhaps most importantly, the 'why' of musicologists would become much clearer if the relationships between musicology and all other aspects of music were better understood. To take a traditional example: a good concert pianist's learning of a musical work and subsequent performance of it is not only the result of a type of musicological study, but also a potential contributor. The musicological component may not be very sophisticated, and involve no direct reading of musicological commentary on the given work by the performer, but it embodies some degree of 'analysis' – often at a subliminal level - that will be influenced by the performer's own training and musicality. The more captivating performances can enrich others' understanding of the composition by clarifying elements of form, tempo, phrasing, etc. as well as by appropriate linking of emotion or mood. If the performance is lucky enough to be in the limelight, it may also receive attention by those who are studying the style and reception of similar works. But the relationship between these aspects is often unacknowledged, and musicology remains for many a closed room whose inhabitants are rarely seen. Moreover, the passion of the musicologists is so rarely expressed overtly in their writings – in keeping with good Western scientific tradition - that other artists (who may not have occasion to meet them in person) sometimes neglect to recognize that passion in their very choice of subject and devotion to their intimate knowledge of it.

5. A Tool Kit for Music Analysis

The field of music analysis has a parallel problem to that of music research in general: it is linked to a bewildering diversity of music and the various means to study, or at least appreciate, each one. A good analyst will naturally choose the most appropriate method for the specific piece or corpus in question. However, there are some often unacknowledged problems:

- both the motivation and the audience for the analysis are likely to be factors in choosing a particular method;

- the ways and means for selecting the most appropriate analytical approach is frequently not discussed, and not always considered;

- the musicologist will probably have a particular skill with or fondness for certain methods – and, inevitably, usually a corresponding lack of expertise for others – which influences the choice; *and*

- the attraction of the piece for any given individual or community may be linked to aspects traditionally implicit or considered too subjective for comment: timbral palette, degree of complexity, rhythmic character, expressive fluctuations of tempo, etc.

The analyst's fondness for certain methods has often been combined with a fondness for the music / era for which the method was developed (i.e. harmonic & formal analysis with Romantic period piano works), in which case there is little dissonance between the two. Nevertheless, many of us spend years looking for adequate tools and language to describe and share what we find particularly fascinating about a piece of music.

Each individual who studies a work of music, or a trend in music, or any other aspect of musicological nature, has a particular motivation for that study. For many people who enjoy music, 'analysis' will not extend much beyond how they 'parse' a work when they listen to it for the first or fiftieth time.[12] However, as soon as the listener begins thinking about how s/he is hearing and 'seeing' a musical work, this is the first step on the analytical trail; conversely, it is rarely mentioned in the more academic analysis at elementary levels, even though it plays a role. A performer may wish to analyze a Beethoven sonata in order to improve his or her performance, whereas a Beethoven scholar might wish to compare it to earlier and later sonatas in order to illustrate a particular maturing in the composer's style. The composition student might wish to study Beethoven's technique in creating a particular texture, and a *mélomane*[13] might hope to gain some insight into the overall formal structure, or the motivating circumstances for the work's composition. It is quite possible that each of these tasks would be best served by a different analytical technique: especially because the depth of exploration may differ considerably, depending on the context. Once the analysis is completed to whatever depth has been chosen, there are other factors that influence our perception of the analysis: is the analyst interested in communicating his/her discoveries to other friends / colleagues? If so, then the means of presentation and dissemination - such as the use of specialized terminology or reference to previous studies - may have a significant impact.

Often, neither the motivation nor an informed choosing of the appropriate angle(s) from which to study the subject is acknowledged. Identifying the motivation is usually quite simple. Choosing the right approach is often

---

12. Parsing: how one encodes information, such as a series of notes. See Ch. 23.

13. I use the term 'mélomane' simply to indicate someone who loves music passionately – perhaps not surprisingly a word without an adequate English equivalent?

much trickier, especially if the individual is not at ease with a variety of strategies and methods (and given the number of approaches, who has the time to master them all?). However, if one is trying to choose an analytical approach for a specific musical or multimedia work, or composer, or performance, then it would be useful to be able to glance at an array of approaches before making one's choice. Additionally, if one is interested in studying use of polyrhythms, or microtonality, it should be easier to trace those compositions which utilize them, along with the extant analytical works that reflect those elements.

I have long tried to imagine what might constitute useful aids to guide potential analysts to select the most appropriate analytical tools and strategies for any particular piece of music from the vast array currently available. Imagine the 19th-century scientist preparing to study an object, armed with various measuring tools (rulers, calipers, weigh scales), magnifying/ enhancing tools (microscopes, infrared glasses), sieves to determine fine-granulated content, swabs to gather samples for the lab, pad & pencil for taking notes. Also, imagine the attention and concentration as s/he moves around the object, standing back, leaning in to examine detail. Although the music analyst may exhibit the same type of attention, it is difficult to imagine tools that would match the immediacy of such physical aids given the ephemeral nature of music. Looking at sonograms and amplitude graphs can help with a few issues, but they don't explain why certain notes or gestures seem to interact in particular ways with other elements of a musical work. They also do not convey much of the information that is vital to remember, dealing with aspects such as the original context of the work (era, genre, function, venue, etc.); the emphasis on one or another parameter, technique, or scale; the particular mood, emotion, memories, associations, etc. that the specific timbres or sonic configurations may evoke in a particular listener. When these issues remain unarticulated and even unconscious, those who are from a different area – or even a different vantage point - can easily mis-read the analysis or be dissatisfied with its findings. In addition, this situation leads to analyses that fail to address the particular attractions of a given musical work; it also leads to an absence of analysis for works that do not make sense by the traditional methods.

One thing that the traditional scientist did in his/her lab was to spend time studying the thing from different angles and distances, with tools that were known for their own usefulness and limitations. In music analysis, however, my feeling has been that the array of tools itself, and the properties and limitations of each, is in need of more deliberate attention. I have therefore been trying to develop a set of resources that I have labelled a *Tool Kit* which might operate as a guide to some recommended analytical techniques, perspectives, research groups, dissemination channels, etc. This kind of information could eventually be distilled into a kind of 'cover sheet' to be appended to any analysis (by the analyst her/himself or by someone else), to enable faster selection of relevant material for a researcher's study. This could read as in *Figure 3*.

This is simply another of many such suggestions which aim to adjust what many of us have perceived as a 'skew' in the emphasis of the musicology and academic communities in general, which has to do with the number and types of analyses that exist in contrast to the number and types of music that exist. Simply put, it has seemed to some of us that the proportion of time and space given to 18th- and 19th-century 'traditional' analyses is overwhelming, especially in undergraduate curricula, given the vast repertoire of music which contain non-tempered tunings, a lack of harmonic complexity, non-orchestral instruments and even natural and electronically-produced timbres, non-binary rhythms and macro-rhythms, sound in non-concert venues, etc. Conversely, the range of methods presented to the music student within core theory and analysis courses are often inadequate to explain the characteristics that can seem most appealing - even when related to traditional musical devices such as rhythmic, timbral, textural, or pitch structures. The link between the specific musical configurations and the emotional response they may trigger is often even more studiously avoided. The necessity of having an aural appreciation is often unstated; this includes not only being able to deduce an optimal performance from a combination of score and recording, but also being able, from a set of instructions, to imagine the aural sounds in one's own head.[14]

The vast array of functions of a specific piece of music – from dance music to accompaniment for prayer - have often been forgotten due to the focus on art music designed to be heard in the concert hall.[15]   All of these attributes - musical aspects and function - are more commonly introduced in 'ethnomusicology' or 'world music' classes, where traditional Western concepts of harmonic and rhythmic structures are more obviously inappropriate. Unfortunately, such courses are not always central to a 'core curriculum' in undergraduate programmes, and even when they are, those aspects of music that are pertinent to analysis may not be identified as such. In addition, their introduction with music that may appear 'foreign' to the

---

14. This is discussed further in Ch. 19 - Notation as an analytical tool.

15. Nowadays, several schools seem to be in a 'backlash' mode, so although they have rectified the undue proportion they have substituted it with a similar proportion of tools still under development, rather than focussing first on how to grasp the essential nature of the music and then choosing an appropriate set of analytical tools.

- *original function:*
    court music
- *subsequent function:*
    film track
- *analysis type used:*
    parametric
- *main focus:*
    phrase structure & harmonic content
- *level of complexity of music*
    low
- *level of analytical detail*
    deep
- *terminology*
    technical
- *deviations from common models:*
    slight

FIGURE 3. 'COVER SHEET' EXAMPLE FOR ANALYSIS

majority of students increases the sense that these are not basic concerns, and their transferability to more familiar music may not be stressed. Meanwhile, jazz and electroacoustic studies develop their own analytical tools, more appropriate to the task at hand, but often not shared outside their classes or applied to Mendelssohn or Boccherini – nor to their favourite pop songs with electronic ingredients or, in increasing numbers of cases, their own culture's musical heritage if different from the dominant.

An initial sketch of my ideas for such a Tool Kit is outlined in Appendix C.

SECTION II:

TOPICS IN

COMPOSITION & ANALYSIS

This section provides an overview of terms and concepts frequently used in (some subfields of) musicology and/or cognate areas, with clarification of how they may be adapted (and hence misunderstood) by different groups. Although most of these are well-understood by most musicians, some of them may never emerge in overt discussion within certain music sub-areas (such as Western Classical 'mainstream' music). Furthermore, non-musicians may not know what some of these terms refer to – nor even some gifted performers, for whom theory classes were dry and irrelevant. In addition, thanks to the long-standing aim of many musicologists to be 'rigorous', topics such as the motivations for composing and the emotional content of music are rarely dealt with. However, in my imagined scenarios, the Conversational Musicologist would need to be fluent with these concepts and be adept at communicating their multiple shades of meaning to other experts.

6. Strategies, motivations, and models for creating art

Musicologists who spend their research time studying composers from the 19th century may well assume that contemporary artists are motivated by the same instincts as their "predecessors". In fact, some of the reasons for making art seem so fundamentally different from those characters (Wagner, Brahms) that some of us don't really think of us as being of the same lineage, at all (see Ch. 3). Some specific and not uncommon motivations for composition include:

- creation of patterns, interesting designs, structures, &/ or forms

- creation of a specific mood, atmosphere, soundscape

- creation of a character or series of characters with certain behaviours; telling a story

- exploration of time and sound

- exploration of rhythms (natural, contrapuntal, complex ratios, speech)

- exploration of pitch (scales, temperament, range, intervals)

- exploration of timbre / timbral possibilities (in general, or of a specific instrument / ensemble)

- expression of conceptual idea(s) - e.g. entropy, circularity, translation

- expression of emotion

- experiments to test one's fluency with newly acquired techniques

- exploration of perception (temporal, aural, multimodal); exploration of memory and its limits (by for ex. variations in rate of presentation or complexity)

- giving a gift to a friend, e.g. a performer, or *via* a

41

performer to a partner

- showing off one's skill; aiming for status / fame
- making money

"Experimental music" became an exceptionally apt term during the mid-20th century: many composers were literally conducting experiments, trying out new devices, strategies, combinations. The term was liberating for some of us: an experiment is not quite a finished product, and therefore exempt from the usual critical reception of a new opus.

Not all compositions of any one composer are likely to fit into a single category from this list, because their motivations may shift with the seasons. Yet there are still many people (usually those who do not associate socially with artists) who assume that only the need for self-expression would explain why one would devote time to making art (rather than money, for example, as the two can seem mutually exclusive).

But this idea of self-expression is a rather 19th-century model, and by extension, the 'expressive artist' analogy can suggest a germ of adolescent self-centredness, and might even imply someone who indulges in histrionics. Expression of inner emotions in general is against the upbringing of many of us (e.g. Scottish Calvinists): being taught not to 'show emotion', being encouraged to avoid indulging in self-centred thoughts. This leads easily to a belief that self-expression in itself is a slightly improper occupation – although it does not hold up to much scrutiny: for example, how would any couple discover that they shared a mutual love if they did not express it somehow? And if a talented musician is able to express grief and despair, might that not be a comfort to a listener who is experiencing something similar?

However, some of us composers prefer to design

patterns and structures in sound more than expressing human emotions, for example. This is partly because we feel that there has already been plenty of attention to humans and their emotions (especially with the poorer copies of Romanticism and Expressionism that snuck into the film and pop music world) and therefore it is refreshing now to have the liberty to spend more time looking at both the natural world and the world of abstract art. As much of the focus of musicological attention has been on urban composers, it seems that those of us fortunate enough to have experienced more natural environments may tend towards Nature as inspiration, as it can provide more sophisticated models than most of the man-made structures, in terms of a composer's favourite elements like subtle unpredictability. Compare the structure of a cave with a suburban house; the fluctuating intensities of a windstorm with rush-hour traffic; the rhythm of footsteps of a hike through a forest with those of a walk down a city sidewalk.[16] Likewise, different cultures favour different emphases: Persian- and Islamic-influenced art, architecture, and artifacts traditionally avoid direct representation – except for sacred texts in calligraphy – and exhibit many complex and refined patterns.

Music is also an excellent medium for exploring intangible things like time, as Xenakis has argued (and demonstrated).[17] I believe he meant this *literally*, not just metaphorically on a conceptual level. He had been

---

16. I found it intriguing that some sidewalks, such as those in Portugal made with small cubes of stone pounded into sand, become uneven with the intervention of tree roots and weather, and as a result are often easier for long-duration walks - less jarring, more comfortable and giving a gentle reminder of the terrain, as well as providing plenty of 'micro-rubato' in the rhythm of footsteps.

17. See for example his comments such as "Music is the sonorous rendering of thought" (Xenakis 1987: 27) and his article "Concerning Time" (Xenakis 1989)

working in engineering and architecture – where one is very tightly constrained by gravitational force and physical characteristics of the materials used – whereas creating works in sound permits the creation of audible structures that can be quite surreal. (A wonderful example of this is Jean-Claude Risset's piece *Invisible Irène*, wherein he presented simultaneously two different acoustic spaces, giving the eerie feeling that one is in two different rooms at the same time.)

There is an oft-quoted phrase "Art for Art's sake" that could be described as an incentive for creating art as a contribution to an ongoing collective exploration, trying to understand cultural attributes and needs, perception, aesthetics, etc. This was a very strong factor in many mid-20th-century art schools in particular, where "Art" meant a certain North American / Western European style, aiming to continue on in the path of the most avant-garde of the recognized artists of the time: from Duchamp to Warhol and Beuys to Smithson. It was rather assumed that (i) these artists were the only ones worth knowing about in the 1960s and '70s; (ii) it would be somehow disloyal to doubt their works as being the best solution to the problems of the day; (iii) forward is the only direction to move (meaning for example that an elegant variant on an existing idea was poorly tolerated, or that a revisiting of 16th century was uncreative); and (iv) there is only one path forward.

In the resulting wake of an overload of shock art and other types striving increasingly desperately to be 'new' and thereby losing the respect of many generally 'cultured' people in society, a different trend emerged, that 'art for art's sake' is a rather elitist stance and no longer acceptable in a responsible society – an opinion as flawed as its predecessor. However, there are many talented musicians who ignore these trends: some jamming with others from different cultures and styles (e.g. classical-jazz, Greek-

Turkish, English Bhangra) some trying to eke out a living by doing things they enjoy (like composing something for a friend's film or puppet show); some who find a good-paying job doing something else, and then create whatever music they want. The results are often highly appreciated by the 30-50 people who hear the results – but rarely make it into the textbooks because they are not marketing themselves in the standard ways, and don't happen to live in the cities where the talent-scouts are active.

It is a very Romantic but (and?) attractive notion to any aspiring composer that any truly excellent music-making will be greeted – eventually – by 'world-wide' acclaim. This model has not been sufficiently adapted to reveal what it always meant – that the 'world' meant 'the community'. In the circles we heard about, that community meant the upper classes of certain cities: Paris, New York, Berlin. But surely it should also stand true for smaller, more remote, or simply less-famous but nonetheless dynamic hubs like "Montreal's experimental dance community" or "music-making in Crete" or "members of Website Collective X". Of course, the idea can also imply, wrongly, that everyone in a specific community will not only share the same, usually unwritten, aesthetic practices but also have the time, patience, and skill to decode the compositional idea. More crucial, but often under-rated by the academics, is that an excellent performance (including acoustics and other environmental aspects – see Ch. 18) and appropriate reception mode on the part of the listener are often necessary prerequisites to the appreciation of any musical work – and these may come late into the composer's lifetime, if not posthumously.[18]

---

18. See for example biographical information on C. Ives or C. Nancarrow

7. The notion of temporal scale (*or:* The zoom factor)

In sculpture, the scale of a work is understood to be quite influential on the piece's reception. Standard considerations are the size of the piece in relationship to humans, and, if applicable, to its real-world counterpart (if it bears some resemblance to a representation of a real-world thing). Things larger than ourselves may be awe-inspiring or intimidating or domineering; things that are smaller than expected may seem precious – partly due to our awareness of how much time and patience were involved in creating a high level of detail in miniature.

In music, the idea of scale is less obvious, but it might be manifest as amplitude, temporal organization, representations of gesture, total duration, etc. Soft and short sonic configurations in Webern miniatures or mixed works of Ching-Wen Chao may well impart a sense of preciousness, where the listener may feel compelled to focus on an unusual degree of detail quite parallel to that of the observer peering into an intricately-carved egg, whereas a loud and extravagant closing gesture played by full orchestra at the conclusion of a Romantic symphony may appear bombastic.

Research into rhythmic perception indicates that much of our sense of "tempo" is related to our own body actions. We seem to interpret the speed of the music to the energy required to move at that speed: in binary-based metric structures, for example, we regard the tempo as "moderate" if it matches what we think of as a 'normal' walking speed, whereas a structure that would require a more energetic walk to track it would be considered fast - with a natural correspondence with ideas of excitement or fear. (Which one of such contrasting emotions can be deduced from other characteristics such as the pitch palette or melodic contour). However, in some cases, the pitch and amplitude may suggest the movements of a smaller or larger than human figure; a very fast movement combined with soft and high sounds, such as in Mendelssohn's *A Midsummer Night's Dream*, may suggest the dancing of "fairy-like" beings, rather than a frantic human. Likewise, a slow movement in a very low register may be employed to represent a slow-moving beast such as the elephant in Debussy's *Jimbo's Lullaby*, rather than the more typical association with a lazy or pensive human.

James Tenney contributed the useful idea of temporal focus in music (1988). For those accustomed to working with digital sound files, the term 'zoom level' is a cogent equivalent, as the zoom tool is essential for navigating through the amplitude or spectral graph representation of a composition – which presents the sound in chronological order and regularity. In the world of images, even old-fashioned cameras and projectors had a 'zoom' function to allow focus on different levels of resolution. In the context of sound, the 'zoom window' will contain a varying number of milliseconds or minutes - perceived usually as corresponding to the timeline of the piece, although at microscopic levels it is grasped more as timbral detail. Tenney's point, as I interpret it, is that the particular level of focus will reveal different aspects, and that the skilled listener should be able to adjust that focus to the most appropriate for the specific passage being heard.[19] He urges us as listeners to become fluent in adjusting the zoom level to focus on detail or larger-scale formal structure at will. This makes a potent analogy for music analysis, because it can suggest various ways of listening to a piece of music. Many musical passages can be

---

19. My thoughts on this matter are detailed in Mountain 2020 and 2022; I have concluded that we usually listen to music on various channels simultaneously, thereby involving multiple foci.

shown to exhibit 'maximum' interest on one or two 'zoom' levels, meaning that the listener who is unable to focus on one of these may 'miss the point'.[20] Classic cases are found in the music of the minimalists such as Reich's *Violin Phase* or passages of 'micropolyphony' by Ligeti where the most lively activity is at the microscopic level, whether in the phase shifts caused by the cyclic dis-alignment and realignment of the live performer's notes with those on tape, or subtle timbral shifts in indecipherable close-knit textures, or the micro-rubato incurred by an exhausted performer repeating the same material over a long period of time. An 'unsuspecting' listener might miss much of the intricate detail of the music by parsing the audio material into much larger chunks than those originally conceived by the composer. In the case of minimalists like Reich, many aspects such as harmonic development were deliberately 'frozen' in order to encourage listeners to shift their attention to a more microscopic level. However, some listeners do not make this shift, thus forming their like or dislike of the piece based on an appreciation of more global attributes such as the specific overall timbre and pitch collection. The optimum zoom level may not only be hard to determine, but depends on the characteristics which the performer has chosen to emphasize, and/or what the analyst (or listener) has chosen to study. If one is interested in the overall harmonic structure of the Reich, then the microscopic level will produce considerable amounts of useless data, as the timbral shifts stay on the same harmonic basis for minutes at a time. Conversely, a randomly-chosen zoom level may reveal detail that prompts a re-evaluation of the characteristics that contribute to a piece's particular charm.

Another factor that influences one's temporal focus is the large-scale formal structure, especially when it

---

20. More discussion of this multiple-focus strategy in Mountain 2020.

48

contains a nesting of metric hierarchies (as in the standard pop song). This has to do with the tracking not only of the beat (if present) and the symmetrical phrase patterns (if present), but also the recurrence, with any perceived degree of regularity, of any feature that seems recognizable – like the theme in a simple *Rondo*.

How should we determine the optimal level for such focus? Is there a single optimal level? or does the piece reveal attractive designs on one level and a compelling message on another? In general terms, analysis should provide some clues; this may be directed by the composer's own comments. However, presumably the 'optimal' level(s) can be deduced by discovering where something interesting is going on. As in many similar situations, this may depend on the particular interests of the listener, may be influenced by the performance, and may shift over the decades or centuries.

8. Parameters: what are they? why do analysts like them? how do they interact?

To a non-musicologist, talk of "parameters" may seem a warning that things are getting technical – the word is rarely used in non-analytical conversations about music. Once it is explained that 'parameters' simply refer to the separate elements of pitch, rhythm, harmony, melody, timbre, and so on, it may appear more reasonable. But the closer one looks, the muddier the waters appear. Many of the parameters are compound,[21] and moreover, there seems to be something greater than the sum of the parameters that makes up a great piece of music. That is to say, music is made up of quite a combination of things, not all of which are easily identifiable - just as paintings cannot be adequately (or even very usefully) described by a technical definition of the colour and thickness of paint and the size of brush.

Parameters in music, as in other fields, are generally an agreed-upon set of definable, measurable characteristics: the aspects of sound-frequency, duration, loudness, etc. that are present in all music but assembled in different ways depending on the circumstances (i.e. the piece, the composer, the style, the era). Perhaps it is a reasonable thing when one is examining something to try to sort it into some sub-categories - and it is further encouraged by Western conventions of written notation (see Ch. 19). Pitch and rhythm (i.e. duration, tempo) are quite clearly described in Western notation – with the limitations described in Chapters 9-10. Therefore, they can be talked about – in classrooms, among musicologists – with considerable precision. "Notice how the V chord goes this time to a minor

---

21. That is, generally heard as one aspect although technically two or more of what we consider 'basic elements' - see Ch. 10.

VI chord – a deceptive cadence, unlike the first iteration of this melody." However, attempts to describe the *character* of a particular melody and its harmonic accompaniment in a mainstream 19th-century work often require recourse to a more picturesque language, thus appearing 'personal' or 'subjective', and as a result are shied away from.

In retrospect, we could say that much of the analytical methods employed in the music classrooms of the 19th century were pitch-based – especially harmonic. In a way, electronic and computer music helped emphasize the various other parameters of music by their realization that to produce any kind of 'melody' on a computer, one needed to specify not only the frequency of the desired pitch and its duration and amplitude, but also the frequency and durations and amplitudes of each of the component harmonics of each pitch, so that there would be some timbral character. Composers such as Stockhausen and Boulez helped reinforce this emphasis in acoustic music (Stockhausen through a direct application of what he had learned in the computer music studio) through a serialization of each of these parameters.

As mentioned, analyzing the parameters in music seems analogous to discussing the materials used by the sculptor, or the colours used by the painter. The problems arise mainly from assuming that by talking about pitch, duration, amplitude, and timbre one will arrive at a full picture of the music. As in most fields, the errors come with what is not articulated: scale, expression, intensity, behaviour, function, context.... What we hear in the music that makes us particularly like or dislike it seem to lie often in the more subtle arrangements that can be much more difficult to identify – and especially to pinpoint in the written score – or in the very obvious ones which are also left out of the discussion.[22] Just as we may grasp the energetic sweep

---

22. Xenakis refers to this phenomenon when he says "There are

of the painter's arm required to produce a certain line on the canvas, which will not be easily described by identifying the colour and direction, so we may be enchanted by the particularly slow fade-out, to a whisper, of a gentle sound that will not be easily identified by pitch or amplitude. And just as we may particularly like paintings that include a certain juxtaposition of pale blue and green, so we may prefer music for clarinet, or in a minor key. Of course the key and the instrumentation will figure somewhere in the preliminary description, but it will not usually receive much analytical attention - because what is there to say? (See Ch. 27.)

A significant problem with parametric analysis is that it suggests to the unsuspecting composition student that these are the materials available for manipulation. Those who are immersed in electroacoustics may find it easier to conceptualize frequency aggregates and layers, but until recently there has been little overlap between electroacoustic and acoustic composition courses. It seems that we should therefore not only review the concept of pitch (see Ch. 9) but also extend the parametric array to include other elements: texture and gesture (see Ch. 13), dissonance levels (Ch. 15), intensity curves, and complexity envelopes.[23]

Intensity curves and complexity envelopes are generally equivalent to what was traditionally understood in terms of phrasing and formal structure. New technologies have

---

sounds which have no pitch, or have so many pitches that you are lost in them, or sounds which do not have one intensity, but are so varying that it's impossible to give them an account, a description." [Zaplitny/ Xenakis 1975])

23. Aspects of these issues are being incorporated by various researchers including Rolf Inge Godøy, Pierre Couprie, and the Marseille-based group Labo-MiM working on the "UST" – Temporal Sound Units.

allowed the study of the microscopic changes in both temporal and amplitude details over the course of a phrase. The temporal detail, known sometimes as 'micro-rubato', has been studied under the term of 'expressive timing'.[24] This research has shown that listeners appreciate the formal structure of a piece, when played by good performers, partly because of "cues" of phrasing: a good performer will naturally slow down towards the end of each phrase, and more so at the end of sections. Although these "mini-ritardandi" are often very slight, and rarely conscious on the part of the performer, our sense of timing is sufficiently acute that we track them. (This is more audible with temporally dense passages: a slowing down is much easier to track in a 'steady' stream of sixteenth notes than with half notes.) It seems evident that similar cues are given by changes in timbre as well as amplitude (and perhaps a bit in pitch, on certain instruments); but such effects have not been sufficiently studied to provide clear means of referring to them.

One reason for exploring this area further is that much post-19th-century music has much less clear phrase structure, but will still benefit from such increases and decreases in these various parameters. If we consider them as curves, profiles, or vectors, and find adequate ways to notate /discuss them, we might benefit not only analysis but composition toolboxes.

---

24. See for example Clarke 1989.

9. Pitch, frequency, temperament, & the piano tuners' union

The concept of pitch is considered absolutely essential to many if not most Western classical musicians and musicologists. The notions of key and scale are also, by extension, basic. It is therefore quite surprising to them when they find other apparently rational musicians for whom the concepts are irrelevant.

To many musicians, 'pitch' is considered almost interchangeable with 'note', as described by letters (from A-G), modifiers ('flat' and 'sharp') and register (whether by specific octave or by the more general relative classifications of high, medium, and low). Moreover, there is a tendency to think of pitches as corresponding closely, if not exactly, to the keys on a piano. However, the piano model immediately limits the reference to (more or less) equal temperament, thus excluding not only most non-Western music but also much that is pre- and post-19th century; it also implies a steady set of frequencies for the entire note's duration, which is atypical in many cases, such as the human voice and all instruments which imitate it.

Common notation reinforces this perspective. Performers often make adjustments to a given, apparently equal-tempered, note according to their desire for expression and/or knowledge of context (usually at a subconscious level), but often the analysts do not take that into account. In some genres, notably electroacoustics but also much expressive vocal music (such as blues and Indian raga), a sound may change (e.g. 'bend') over the course of its duration. When this is a prevalent characteristic, the whole term of 'pitch' becomes less useful. In electroacoustics, it is sometimes replaced by descriptions of the changing of the frequency complex, for which the term *spectromorphology* has been much appreciated (see Smalley, 1986).

Most of us are extremely sensitive to slight differences in pitch when we learn to recognize speech, but many attributes of current Western music de-sensitize people to a similar discrimination in music contexts.[25] On the other hand, a typical music history survey generalization, in my day, was that most non-Western music did not manage to "reach the sophistication of harmonic complexity" without acknowledging that the apparent trade-off - abandoning the subtle shadings of diverse tunings, timbres, and rhythms - was not necessarily a clear advantage. The blame is of course not with the music but the professors and textbooks, because there is plenty of Western music with subtle shadings of pitch, timbre, and rhythm as well – as well as large quantities of 'early' music with less harmonic complexity - but it is poorly represented in notation and (therefore?) frequently ignored.[26] In any case, the lack of sophisticated notation to clarify any tuning other than equal temperament has been one of the main factors hindering analysis of music for which temperament is a crucial factor. Similar situations exist for rhythm and timbre - their notation is clumsy, subtle, or non-existent and therefore often escapes the score-reader.

It is interesting to note that in the ancient (and very sophisticated) musical traditions of India and Persia, for example, the notion of scale is replaced by similar (but not synonymous) ones of raga (India) and dastgah (Persia). These systems also indicate a fairly precise collection of notes, with registral repetition, but with three distinct

---

25. This is quite different for those who, like myself, listened extensively to non-tempered music at early age.

26. Furthermore, it can be argued that one can hear harmonic complexities in Indian music, for example, in certain listening modes that widen the temporal 'now' to a longer passage than is typical for Western traditions.

differences. First of all, the pitches are not considered 'steady-state' but are each potentially associated with a particular 'gamaka' (Indian) that indicates a bend or ornament at the beginning of the particular note, or on an improvisatory detailed vibrato.[27] Therefore, a basic set of pitches may belong to more than one raga, but due to the particular gamakas, the ragas will be differentiated. Secondly, although certain key pitches (tonic, major third, perfect fourth) may be stable from piece to piece, the other notes may be altered within a certain margin, chosen by the performer for a particular "colour" or mood.[28] Thirdly, the traditions indicate not only the collection of notes to be used, but also something of the order; the most familiar aspect of this to Westerners is the possibility of an 'ascending' and a 'descending' version of the melodic minor scale, but this is not used so widely within the music itself; a closer correlate is found in the typical patterns of Baroque counterpoint.

A major reason for electroacoustic music being so studiously ignored by "mainstream" textbooks and musicologists is probably due precisely to its lack of notation and lack of familiar concepts like pitch. For a composer of musique concrète, for example, producing a discrete pitch sequence either in the analogue studio or through recordings of disparate objects and events is usually bland and/or extremely difficult; moreover, it is unnecessary to the conceptualization of a good musical piece. In the studio, one could hook up an oscillator and, by ear or by consulting a frequency chart, dial a succession of numbers that reproduce a familiar scale. But in order

27. Not to be confused with "tahrir", a Persian term for a vocal tremolo technique whereby the sound flow is repeatedly interrupted but the exact pitch stays the same.

28. And possibly shaped by the acoustics of the performance venue: one potential aspect of the introductory presentation of the raga.

to produce a 'nice, rich sound', a few more oscillators would be required to fade in and out at some points to produce the overtones (harmonics) common to all natural instruments and sounds, which we therefore expect in a "lifelike" sound. Alternatively, imagine that a composer has some recordings of a couple of metallic objects, some dice being thrown onto a drum, a train clattering on the tracks, a robin (slowed down to quarter-speed) and some waves on the beach. To try to associate these with specific pitches would be very taxing. On the other hand, it is easy to be sensitive to their characteristic frequency range (broad/narrow, high/medium/low) and remain alert to any sense of pitch or harmony imparted by any one of them, to exploit or avoid apparently 'tonal' implications. But most of all, the electroacoustic composer will likely be more concerned with the general 'character' and 'behaviour' of the sounds in order to arrange them into 'meaningful' or expressive forms.

For compositions with clear utilization of the pitch concept, the term *pitch collection* can be a convenient alternative to *scale*, to denote the pitches chosen by a composer for a given passage or 'layer' of music. In other words, a composer or improviser is likely to employ a subset of the (conceptually) available pitches (12, in equal temperament) for any given passage. Notes outside of this set may be used in ornamental ways, such as grace notes, but conceptually those are thought of not as full-fledged members of the set but rather as ornament to a specific note, just as gamakas are in Indian music. This subset will be chosen to lend a certain character to the passage, analogous to the palette of colours used by a painter. In 18th- and 19th-century European classical music, such subsets usually coincided with a major or minor scale, but in the 20th century, or in other cultures, they may be less evenly distributed. This is especially true in complex passages where the composer is creating the illusion of two or more "layers" of music; for perceptual reasons, it is more efficient to have less overlap of pitches between layers.

Range and timbre are also extremely important in perception; an interval C-E in a very high register is not necessarily perceived as closely related to the same interval several octaves lower; this dissimilarity is heightened when the intervals are played by different instruments. This brings up another problem with the pitch concept, which was thrown into highlight by the oddly-persistent phenomenon of 12-tone music in the 20th century. Pitches are usually regarded, by traditional Western musicians and analysts, first of all as notes that repeat cyclically by octave. Therefore, the parallels between each of the 12 notes of the chromatic scale in any octave are usually considered stronger than their registral differences. Transpositions - the shifting up and down from one set of notes to another with the same intervallic distance - are equally considered to be less transformative compared to those of changing the order of pitches, for example. And in much Western music from the 19th century, this is indeed the case. To some extent, this is because melodies would not be transposed into very high or very low registers, due to a long tradition inspired by an innate understanding of acoustics, human perception, and sound production (e.g. the natural tendency of males to sing a song one or two octave lower than the females in a group). However, these factors were often ignored by dodecaphonic and serialists, with the result that the "row" was often obscured by registral and timbral variety. Of course, this does not indicate any flaw in the design - composers should be free to use any device they wish to produce their art, and early serialists were exploring new ways to arrange sounds - but it does indicate that an analysis that focusses on the row may be somewhat misleading if it does not clarify the relative importance of the device to the result.

Another interesting point is the number of main pitches used in any given piece: many musics of the world traditionally restricted these to 5, 6, or 7 notes per octave, regardless of the intervals. It may suggest that the psychologists' 'magical number 7' operates also in this sphere; that music staying with 7 (+/-2) different notes could be an optimum number for recognition.[29] Hence the use of 12 notes in a single passage of music (e.g. serial) can be appreciated as being taxing on the brain trying to organize the sounds.[30]

Nonetheless, it would be foolish to assume that we should abandon the concept of pitch and insist on a more modern vocabulary that substitutes gestures, textures, frequencies, and spectra, as it *is* perfectly useful in some situations even outside harmonic contexts. But it can be interesting to reflect on its usage. Gestures and textures tend to be used at a larger (slower) temporal grouping level than pitch, while frequency and spectrum tend to be at quite a small (faster) level. This may mean that those who work with pitch tend to be focussing on a level of temporal detail intermediate between that of their colleagues in the electroacoustic world. Does this continue upwards? Do pitch-based composers tend to group pitches into longer groups than electroacoustic composers do with their gestures?

---

29. The term 'magical number 7 plus or minus 2' was first used by Miller in 1956 to refer to short-term memory and information, and seems to crop up in various contexts in human cognition. It is interesting to contemplate if this range of 5-9 also extends to the optimum number of distinct ideas in a musical work.

30. This might imply, by extension, a disastrous situation for electroacoustics, but composers in that field will point out that pitch is substituted by recognizable conglomerates or aggregates of a similar size set.

10. Timbre, articulation, amplitude, and spectromorphology

As mentioned in Ch. 8, there are several cases of 'compound' parameters not always implicit in the labelling. Articulation, amplitude, and timbre, for example, are inextricably linked. This was inadvertently brought to the attention of some by Boulez in his *Structures Book I*, which Ligeti pounced on (1960) for its ignoring of these fundamental principles. Boulez separated (and serialized) articulation, dynamics, and timbre (that is, the different registers of the piano) with ludicrous results, giving impossible directions such as a *sforzando pianissimo*, or a *fortissimo* in the very high register where it is impossible to produce a note of such volume.

One of the obstacles to appreciating the effect of articulation on timbre is the rather vague definition of timbre which serves many non-electroacoustic musicians: "It's the difference between the sound of a flute, a piano, and a violin". In fact, timbre also describes some of the difference between a flute playing a high note and a low note, and between playing each soft and loud. A further hindrance to the discussion is that our perception tends to combine these elements, so that the majority of people asked to comment between a soft and loud flute note will focus on the amplitude, relegating the timbral qualities to an unspecified by-product. As it becomes increasingly easy to show high-quality spectrograms of any given recorded sound, perhaps these changes that affect the relative strength of the component harmonics can be more easily demonstrated and understood.

The existence of harmonics themselves can be one of the most difficult concepts to explain to music students and non-musicians alike, as it involves needing to acknowledge that sounds that have been happily thought of as single notes are in fact composites. In fact, the most effective way to demonstrate it seems to be with recourse to examples manipulated in the auditory perception laboratories where a note is repeated several times with various harmonics supressed, or manipulated. These changes are perfectly audible to all music students and most non-musicians – and therefore easily identified as timbral - but still difficult to reconcile with our ideas of what a note is. On the other hand, our dissatisfaction with any but the most sophisticated software for synthesizing voices is related exactly to these parameters.[31]

These factors contribute to a lack of sophisticated terminology for describing timbre – and therefore contributing to a lack of sensitivity to its manipulation, in a kind of vicious circle. Many 20th-century scores – especially from the mid-century - are replete with very precise indications of articulation as a way of exacting timbral shifts (see for example some of Berio's). A more subtle but often equally or even more effective means is to tell the performer what mood or character should be conveyed (e.g. 'melancholy', or 'mechanical and brittle') as this will allow the performer to make micro-adjustments to a range of parameters – tempo, amplitude, articulation, etc. – without having to think about each one separately. However, this works only when the passage represents only one or two 'characters' - otherwise, it becomes too confusing for the performer. These two systems serve relatively well for instructing the performer, but leave the analyst without any particular way of describing the results. Timbral classifications and schema are still rare, although the challenge was issued a century ago by Russolo,

---

31. Although I believe the trend is for people who listen extensively to radio and television commentators to become less discriminating, as the filtering of voices to portray more authority becomes increasingly pronounced.

whose *Art of Noise* – a Futurist manifesto often referred to in electroacoustic classes – categorized noises in ways proposed as useful for musical manipulation. (Fortunately, researchers such as Stephen McAdams at McGill University have been creating fertile ground for promoting the work of different pioneers through recent conferences and projects.)

There is another curious phenomenon that may contribute to our glossing over of timbre: we are encouraged to recognize melodies, for example, regardless of their key, register, and instrumentation. This is doubtless a natural tendency - somewhat akin to recognizing verbal phrases regardless of the speaker's accent or gender. But because it is reinforced by the analysis teacher urging students to identify the recurrence of melodies and other pitch configurations that may articulate the main sections of a musical work, the student is nudged into regarding the timbre as less important. On the other hand, if one were to examine each melodic recurrence in light of the subtle variations provided by instrumentation - the way one might for tracing the evolution of a leitmotif - then the timbre and register would be more appreciated, as we should assume that the composer does not pick instrumentation at random. The piano also contributes to the "suppression" of timbre as a defining force because many 19th-century composers would write for piano, for reasons of convenience and marketability, and although they could produce different timbres with the particular configurations of texture density, pitch collection, and register, these are considerably more subtle than the differences of bowed violin and plucked cello – and more likely to be under-emphasized by an amateur performer or even an excellent performer playing on an upright in the living room.

Amplitude is another aspect of music that seems perfectly clear unless one is a composer trying to create subtle shifts of amplitude in a piece. There are three main problems:

- the notational system that assigns "*ppppp*" to "*fffff*" is not sufficiently nuanced around the mid-range (probably because the range itself expanded over the centuries), but the mid-range is probably where we are most able to make fine discrimination;

- the notational system is interpreted in a relative and not an absolute fashion by performers – there is no innate measure for how loud an '*mf*' really is; and

- when one is writing for more than one instrument, it is not always clear whether the indications in the score mean the same thing for each instrument, or whether they refer to the overall resultant sound.

Traditionally, this last point is solved by the conductor in a large ensemble, and by the players themselves in a smaller one, so that if everyone in the orchestra has an '*mf*', then the conductor knows that the oboes may need to 'come down' a bit, the violas play a little louder, etc. – just as she or he will adjust the levels to compensate for the acoustic properties of the venue. Problems arise, however, when there are two or more ideas being presented simultaneously. Imagine that some of the ensemble is portraying a musical layer that is creeping in from inaudibility, while the others are playing a passage that is fading away. When the ideas are sufficiently clear to all, then this can be accomplished easily – but when it becomes complex (imagine that the violins shift from one layer to another) the composer ends up having to indicate very precise dynamics (which is impossible, due to their relative indications) and the performers often become overwhelmed by the amount of information on the score.

It is useful to recognize that what is often called 'expressive' performance implies considerable dynamic

63

modulation – that is, subtle shifts in amplitude. At the very basic level, this involves a tapering off of sound at the end of a phrase – just like its analogy in much spoken language. However, if the particular musical language becomes less clear, the performer(s) may not know what or where the 'phrase' is, where it ends, etc.

It is this kind of problem that drives some composers back to the electroacoustic studio, where we can make exactly the type of modulation we wish (although sometimes with difficulty, or at least with an inordinate investment of time).

11. The voice and the drum

It is quite compatible with the academic study of music to consider the voice as "just another instrument". However, when one studies the ancient traditions of Indian or Persian music, one discovers that the voice is generally considered primary, and much of the instrumental repertoire evolves from its imitation. This lineage may be a crucial factor in a general appreciation of music. We are highly tuned to recognizing the various nuances of a voice as carriers of emotion, and therefore it is natural that people began to transfer some of those aspects effectively to instruments in order to evoke similar effects to songs.[32] Bowed instruments with skin stretched over a resonating chamber - such as the rabab and kamancheh ('spike fiddle') - seem particularly capable of emulating such vocal qualities as tremor and breath variations, though wind and brass players are also able to use their instruments as complex megaphones for timbrally-altered vocal sounds. Various studies clarify how the nuances of rhythmic phrasing can be understood as relating to the rhythms of speech - different language bases producing different rhythmic structures (cf. Bartók). It is true that we often hear instructions from the instrumental teacher that refer to these qualities: "Make that phrase sing!" just as we also use performance instructions that refer to human mood: "melancholy", "allegro [cheerful]" etc. But many of us Western musicians trained in the 20th century have forgotten these connections.

Meanwhile, aspects of 'steady' rhythm such as drumming relate very directly to dancing and other human activities – even a synthesized drum-beat can imply the drumming action to anyone who has ever held two sticks and played with them. A logical conclusion from these two

---

32. In fact, a striking idea is presented in Mithin's *The Singing Neanderthals*, which posits that song came before speech.

associations – voice and limb movement – suggests that listeners of music will be conditioned by what they know from their own bodies - and the voices and bodies of family and friends - about voice and movement.

Humans also invented instruments to imitate birds and animals for reasons of hunting, and possibly to establish communication with them - or simply to blend into an environment. (Note for example the bone flutes found in Germany dating from 40,000 B.C.E.) It must also have been useful to be able to evoke the impression of different environments and phenomena – water, thunder, rockslides – for which the strumming of strings could also be quite effective, along with an array of percussion instruments which can be constantly expanded with found objects. Such depictors of sonic characters would not just enhance the telling of tales; they might be able to contribute essential information more effectively than words.

The advent of electronic instruments has been linked in part to the parallel wish to depict a modern urban environment. And while some modern composers like to feel 'above' such primitive motivations, and free to combine any sound-producers without thinking about their historical derivations, it could be useful to re-introduce discussion of these attributes in order to clarify intentions and retain a sense of what are probably latent universal reactions.

12. Musicians as time-smiths and rhythmicists

Time is a main element in music; it is our 'medium' just as a sculptor's medium might be stone or steel. However, we don't seem to talk much of time *per se* - probably because it is regarded in so many different ways. Even our perception of pitch is time-dependent: when the orchestra tunes to "concert A" it is usually 444 cycles per second, and if someone is heard playing 438 cycles per second, s/he is considered "out-of-tune." (Non-musicians may not be quite so perceptive in these small discriminations, yet they may grasp a "sloppiness" of tuning and regard it as typical of a high school ensemble, for example, without knowing why.) The same applies to tiny differences in "attack" on a chord; a few milliseconds' difference between notes of a chord played by several fingers on the piano or by several members of an ensemble may convey a sense of 'sloppiness'. On the other hand, a good pianist will often play one of several notes in a chord a couple of milliseconds "early" in order to attract attention, for example to a note that is part of a melodic line, thus separating its function from the other accompanying notes. (This is studied within the 'expressive timing' research strand.) Very few performers will actually think of such things in terms of millisecond differences, but will nonetheless master the technique to do so.

An example of a terminology hindrance to the flow of research findings between music researchers and those in psychology is the expression of temporal units. Musicians, especially those using composing or recording technologies, often use frequencies for audible pitches, clusters, bands, etc. – but for rhythmic concerns, if using notation, will think in terms of beats per minute and their subdivisions (sixteenth notes, etc.) whereas the psychologists use milliseconds when describing the distance between the attack of notes in a series, and use Hz. (beats per second) for discussion of motor movement clocks, brainwaves, etc. This is unfortunate, because there are clearly links between our inner clocks and our response to specific tempi and other periodicities in music. But what performer is willing to, or able to, count milliseconds?[33] Nonetheless, composers and performers do need to present the music through many minutes, if not hours, with at least some attention to each millisecond and its context even though at a subliminal level.

Duration, which is a key concept in time studies, is also used in a very narrow and sometimes misleading way in normal discourse around composition and performance, as we call the length of notes 'durations' but rather than giving them a straightforward millisecond equivalence, for example, they are measured in terms of the selected beat, whose clock-time equivalence (in the form of metronome marking, seconds, or vaguer instructions such as allegro, is established at the beginning of the passage (and may be constantly modified by *ritardandi* or *rubato*, for example).

A composer may consider time in various ways:

- how long will the piece last? how long do I want it to appear to last? will it be clearly sectionalized or a more fluid transition between different parts? if sections, how many? even or uneven durations?

- what is the density of activity in a passage? (i.e. how many notes or how much activity per unit of duration?) Is the density constant or dynamic? If dynamic, is it changing in a in a regular (predictable) or irregular way?

---

33. There are performers who have an excellent innate sense of durational ranges to millisecond precision, but it is usually thought of – by the performer and the listener – only in a general sense of having a 'good sense of timing'.

- is there a sense of beat? if so, how fast? Is the tempo produced constant or fluctuating? If fluctuating, in a regular (predictable) or irregular way?

- is there a sense of meter? if so, what is it? is it constant or dynamic? if dynamic, is it changing in a in a regular (predictable) or irregular way?

- how are things grouped? by a hierarchical nesting of meters or by a more additive approach?

- what will be the most typical listening mode / level of attention? how can I affect it? which elements do I want to be memorable? how many times will each idea return?

- is the performer permitted / encouraged to modulate the timing on a micro- and/or macro-level?

The composer may think about the overall duration of a phrase, passage, section, or entire piece as a section of time to be shaped by arranging its various components. Thus the consideration of density of activity is operating at several levels. The order in which one can look at each "level" of organization is dependent on the particular piece (and therefore may be influenced by the material itself, the piece's destination, and/or the composer's particular state of mind).

We have a sense of a "norm" in periodic movement based on our experience of typical limb movement in a relatively "normal" manner; fast and slow are thus usually perceived in relation to that. (See also discussion of 'scale' in Ch. 7.) The composer may think of the temporal organization of a composition likewise in terms of its similarity or deviation from his/her perception of "normal" time as experienced in daily life. Pieces composed in the environment of ocean soundscapes, for example, may seem unduly "slow" when heard in a large city, where the urban pace is considerably more frantic.

CONCERT / CD STRUCTURE: Exactly the same sense of temporal organization occurs when the person organizing a concert or festival structure, or the producer of a CD, chooses the order of the various pieces. If these pieces are not by the same composer, the composer generally relinquishes control over that order. In the case of concerts especially, when thought is given to the order, it will likely be for other important factors such as the physical exertion and mental focus required by the performers: the hardest piece should not be first, but if it is last and preceded by other complicated ones, then it may suffer from a poor performance. As a result, the effect of the order on the listener's pacing is often relegated to a lower priority. However, one's sense of time will always be affected by full concentration on a musical work, especially when it reaches 15-20 minutes in length. The rate of information and the specific tempo – whether a noticeable beat or not, and the length of the phrases – will cause most listeners to have latent expectations for the subsequent piece, as a pause of a few minutes is not enough to cancel a slow rhythmic ebb & flow.[34]

ADDITIVE RHYTHMS: It seems that an additive approach to rhythm was once used by many cultures, but has been largely superseded by metric organization in European and Western music in general. It suggests a way of composing that is distinct from a sense of meter and hypermeter. Examples abound in J. S. Bach as well as Prokofiev, Shostakovich, Lutoslawski, Bartók, etc.

Additive rhythm indicates that a rhythmic pattern or organization is constructed by the linking together of several (usually very small) rhythmic units, often repetitions or variations of a single cell. Additive rhythm

---

34. This is as likely to be manifest a need for contrast in the 'texture' of the time, rather than a continuation of a very similar temporal structure from one piece to another.

is significantly different from metric rhythm as a way of approaching rhythmic organization - although it is possible to arrive at some identical structures from the two different approaches. It is generally much more organic in nature, and introduces variation very simply. A pattern "long-short-short-short" can be extended to "long-short-short-short-short" or reduced to "long-short-short" without losing its identity - but the resulting sense of metric structure will be fundamentally altered. Bartók uses this device frequently in works such as his String Quartets to create tension (in the case of truncation). Semiotic analysis [à la Nattiez] can provide clear diagrams of such structures.

Illustrations of additive rhythm popularized by Messiaen are a subset of the larger category; he focussed on a particular multiplication factor to construct his patterns: lengthening individual notes by 50% or interpolating a short note into an otherwise regular rhythm (a classic example is 'Danse de fureur' from the *Quatuor pour le Fin du Temps*), or using rhythmic cells alternating between two and three units. Shostakovich has many good examples of irregular phrase lengths in his works, such as the string quartets. This irregularity can be clearly sensed, but is less visible in the score when the bars are all or mostly the same length; one has to resort to counting the specific durations in what are often parallel phrases.

Additive rhythms can easily approximate an improvisation feel. Metric schemes imply a pre-planning, on auditive as well as cognitive levels: the scheme is established and deviations are able to be interpreted as significant due to the regularity of the underlying macrostructure. With additive rhythm, however, there is little or no assurance about the exact duration of the phrase, just a sense of its nature and pace. A pulse is often maintained, that substitutes for the bar and phrase as the regularity index. The virtuosity of Indian musicians in the *tala* section depends on the soloist's ability to retain a large-scale structure in the head within which all the (often unequal) sub-phases must fit. However, in an *alap* session, such predictable phrase lengths are not usually found.

Hypermeter is a term used to indicate the hierarchical arrangement of measures that form a regularity that approximates meter on a higher (longer-duration) level. It is a fine concept, but is rarely found in any extensive usage outside dance forms (where a regularity of phrase structure is crucial for group dancing where a dance is learned independent of a specific musical work) - Boccherini's famous *Minuet* is a classic example. Many composers in Western tradition have used the techniques of elision and prolongation to add variety to an otherwise hyper-metrically organized (and therefore rhythmically predictable) piece. This may result in uneven phase lengths and occasionally changes in time signature. However, a proliferation of time signatures in a piece may give a clue that additive rhythm has been used in the piece's conception. In fact, an additive approach is quite typically used in Western music at the level of mid- to large-scale form.

FORMAL STRUCTURE: The design of large-scale formal structures is essential a question of how the temporal framework is conceived. There are many templates available: binary, sonata form, rondo, narrative, minimalism, multiple layers, mapping natural phenomena (see Ch.13). Each of these implies a different "flow" of time: an oscillation between two states; the telling of a tale in which the characters evolve; an almost static texture; a constant recurrence of an idea. Some composers, myself included, prefer to invent new forms, but this is risky because the listener will have fewer expectations and then need more guidance in how to track the time at the proper rate. My solution is in part to present interesting material with different internal rhythms and densities so that the listener will have something interesting to follow regardless of which level of activity is chosen for focus – rather like a landscape painting where the observers can choose to study different aspects in their own time.

The relationship of music and time, and the ways in which we can and might discuss it, is to me one of the most fascinating and under-explored topics in the field of music. I have therefore devoted an entire book to this one topic.[35]

---

35. Mountain 2022.

13. Gestures, textures, and other nice complexities

GESTURE: Although many musicians are at ease with the term 'musical gesture', it turns out that different people apply quite distinct meanings to it. As it is rarely defined in music textbooks, this variety of meanings has long escaped notice.

The interpretations seem to fall into the following broad categories:

- the sonic result (or 'trace') of a physical gesture, such as: the strum of a guitar, the strike of a stick on a drum;

- the sonic imitation of a physical gesture, such as 'a rising gesture';

- a more or less formal musical pattern used to suggest a particular idea; for example: the 'opening gesture' or 'closing gesture' of a work;

- abstract / conceptual - the composer and/or analyst surmises that a certain musical idea indicates a type of syntactical punctuation in the composition.

Investigation into type (a) gesture is now gaining considerable momentum because of research into gestural controllers for musical instruments.[36] This is also fairly closely related to type (b), as the link between a physical gesture and the resulting sound is considered essential for an "intuitive" controller.[37]

In the context of analysis, the term 'gesture' seems most useful when relating to a relatively short and distinct sonic configuration; what Smalley has called an "energy

---

36. See for example Wanderley & Battier 2000.

37. However, this research requires more work on mapping (see Ch. 14).

trajectory." In a "normal" state, a gesture will be short, probably framed by silence, and implies a continuity of simple, traceable movement -- just like a typical physical gesture of the hands/arms. The implication of movement can also be understood as the (single) action resulting from a single energy burst. This unity of movement may be conveyed by the linear or logarithmic organization of one or more of the parameters: thus, an ascending line of pitches; a steady *crescendo-decrescendo* pattern of amplitude; a series of increasingly long durations; etc. It can convey mood once its identity is established, just as a hand-wave can express eagerness, boredom, or sadness. This gives it some parallels with the *Leitmotiv*, but the latter has a more precise definition, historical usage, an implicit association with melody, and is often much longer and/ or complex. Work by Godøy and others[38] is helping researchers understand gesture as links between music and our perception of the physical world.

TEXTURE: The term 'musical texture' had a significantly different meaning in the 18th-19th centuries to that which it gained in the 20th - although there are conceptual links. In earlier times, the term referred to the specific way of arranging the various different 'voices' in a passage; the second usage was not well defined for so many years that there still exists confusion and a degree of ambiguity. This confusion is also due to the familiarity of the term in its non-musical usages with a lack of clarity in the relationship between that association and the musical usage: the texture of a physical surface, or, in the image world, an abstract patterning.[39]

---

38. E.g. Godøy & Leman, 2010.

39. In dance, the term can refer to an imagined medium other than air, so that a choreographer can suggest a movement as if through sand, or through oil, or through water, that will convey to the dancer the degree of resistance to be implied.

Likewise, some people, with a tendency to cross-modality, have strong associations with words like "sharp", "bright" "coarse" and "rough" which they then expect to hear in any musical texture with those descriptors. Interviews with Ligeti contain several examples of such cross-modal descriptors. Acousticians have developed a very specific vocabulary to describe characteristics of sounds, but the problem is that very few non-specialists know that usage, and therefore the more imaginative will expect to find a close resemblance between their own perception of the sound and their own perception of the visual aspects alluded to by the term.

In a general sense, musical texture refers to the temporal and registral distribution of notes in any given passage. Sparse texture consists of few notes per time unit, and/or spread over a wide registral range, where each component can be heard individually. Dense texture is composed of many notes sounding close together in time, and/or compressed into a limited portion of the registral range. Most typically, the identification of texture applies to a relatively dense backdrop to a melodic line. This is precisely analogous to the figure/ground relationships of the two-dimensional field, and the perceptual issues correspond to those developed by Gestalt psychologists to explain visual perception.[40]

In more traditional musical language, texture has been described generally in terms of homophony, polyphony, and heterophony.[41] Thus, 'texture' refers to the specific nature of the component parts according to common configurations.

Although there are correspondences between these

---

40. Erickson (1975) was one of the first musicians to describe textures in this way.

41. Berry [1976] provides excellent detailed descriptions.

two usages, their resemblance is not at all obvious, as the traditional usage refers to codified means of note distribution, and the student may not grasp how to apply the words to more contemporary music.

Musical texture may be hard to describe accurately because it involves thinking about sound spatially. Rather than a musical line, melody, or gesture that has a beginning and an end, a musical texture can be heard as a distribution of sounds in 'space' - what music theorists call a 'linear pitch-space', where register is an integral component. Musical textures usually have a minimum duration of several seconds, and may last for several minutes (or hours, in extreme cases). However, listening to a musical texture can give the sensation of timelessness, because the sense of movement connected to melodies or gestures is not necessarily present in musical textures. In other words, they often appear as more static than dynamic, unlike melodies and harmonic 'progressions'. There are changes in almost all musical textures, over a course of seconds or minutes, because otherwise the composer would risk the listener's boredom. But the changes are usually more gradual, and cover a wider range of sounds moving in linked form, or confined to small levels of activity at the more immediate level.

It is therefore critical in inter-disciplinary discourse to identify the particular usage of such terms, and to discover similarities, if any, between the musical and non-musical uses of the term.

MULTIPLE STRATA: Some of us are fascinated by passages that have more than one musical "idea" presented simultaneously. These can be found in many eras of music (such as in Mozart opera), but several seminal works of the 20th century are characterized by such behaviour - even in the absence of the cues presented by spatially-distant groups of singers or other performers. The ear can focus on different 'layers' or 'strata', each of which has a distinct identity, and the results can simulate the effect of listening to a three-ring circus or urban soundscape: clear examples can be found in larger acoustic works by Stravinsky, Ives, Messiaen, Xenakis, Lutoslawski and Varèse, and are particularly characteristic of electroacoustic music, where in fact much less 'sleight-of-hand' is required, as different layers can be composed and registered independently. In all of these cases, there exists a sense of design which parallels that of counterpoint, but on a higher level of abstraction: a "counterpoint of strata". There seems a link between the presentation of multiple strata in music with the celebration of multiple, diverse coexisting events, cultures, time-frames, and the like which characterize many perspectives developing since the early twentieth century. Lutoslawski's *Concerto for Orchestra*, for example, presents a rather chaotic design of different entries of melodies and gestures which never synchronize with each other or the regular passacaglia background; this might feel disorienting for some listeners who prefer a more artificial structuring of life, but which delights some ears.[42]

Composers through the ages have enjoyed the challenge of arranging complex ingredients into pleasing formations, or using complex structures to organize elements. As these complex solutions are sometimes inaudible, revealed only through the lens of a particular analytical tool, some might wonder why they are employed. There are three likely causes:

- some composers believe that music is a good medium for revealing some of the natural structures of our universe by replicating their proportions into the realm of the audible - e.g. music of the spheres;

---

42. A fuller discussion of this work can be found in my Ph.D. dissertation (Mountain 1993)

- some composers simply like puzzles, and enjoy working them out in the context of music;
- some composers enjoy using "non-musical" structures to replace certain steps taken by tradition or intuition.

This last reason is sometimes as doomed to failure as it sounds: the composer can't figure out how to develop a passage, and therefore relies on a framework that has its own integrity, to substitute for his/her own lack of solutions. However, other cases are much more valid (as with Schoenberg and Cage): the composer may wish to force him-/herself away from the tendencies of tradition, to discover new potentials; or recognize that certain parameters are not central to the imagined form, and therefore choose an external source of organization to act not as a "time-saver" but as a trigger for new approaches to the artform.

14. Mapping, isorhythms, and other composers' hobbies

MAPPING: Mapping, in musical contexts, refers to the designing of musical material (usually an entire passage or piece) by modelling it on non-musical data. This can be done in a number of ways, ranging from very free to very constrained.

A free version is to use a mood or phenomenon as inspiration for compositional design: this could include Vivaldi's (and others') *Four Seasons*, where the perceived character of the season will provide the composer with ideas for the choice of harmonies, instrumentation, melodic character, etc. This overlaps with musical imagery – a fascinating field studying the compositional strategies of some composers.[43] The constrained version of mapping is when the composer determines a particular relationship between a set of data and musical parameters. An early example of this is Dodge's *Earth's Magnetic Field*, where the composer chose the data of earthquake activity in a specific place in California for one year, and then assigned the various peaks and troughs to frequency and amplitude; the year's data was compressed to a short time period but retained its precise temporal order. In such an approach, the composer does not actually have to 'compose' the piece after making such decisions, but can hand it over to a computer and assistant, as the mapping is a fixed relationship. Often, however, the end result can be much less compelling than the process: for example, in the Dodge work, the resulting timbres can become tiring, whereas the sonorities in Xenakis's works reveal that his particular assignment of data to musical parameters are more carefully

---

43. My first investigation into composers' use of musical imagery can be found in Mountain 2001.

chosen for their aesthetics. However, inevitably, much of the talk about works based on such systems focusses on the system and not the actual results of the mapping of the data (see Ch. 32 for more discussion of this tendency). Works that fall between these extremes would include Cage's *Atlas Ellipticalis* and Honegger's *Rugby*. Honegger's *Pacific 231*, reminiscent of a train, was apparently not his idea for title or impetus; Villa Lobos' *Little train of the Caipira*, however, is a deliberate musical representation of a train struggling uphill and then racing downhill again - thus a type of mapping, though the timeline is necessarily realistic to enable recognition of the moving image.

Xenakis and Stockhausen both indicated a use of mapping in referring to natural rhythms as models or at least analogic to musical passages.[44] The crucial points are not *what* information is used as much as *how* it is 'mapped' – as mentioned above – and at what particular 'zoom' level. Will one map 5 minutes or a year's worth of data onto 5 minutes or 25 minutes of music? It is an excellent exercise for composition students, in conjunction with a reflection on what makes an interesting formal structure.

In more recent times, the practice of mapping has led to sonification, which means to use sounds to make data more easily grasped – such as the level of activity on a web server. In such cases, the musical value of the result is irrelevant – but the mapping activity still has to be done carefully so that the sonic effect reflects the appropriate degree of change.

ISORHYTHMS ETC.: Isorhythm is a device already known in the "Middle Ages": a series of pitches is repeated many times, each assigned to a duration according to an

---

44. Different but related explorations of natural rhythms have been explored by others such as Annea Lockwood in her *World Rhythms* (1975) where natural sounds in their wildly different native time-frames are juxtaposed.

independent series of rhythmic durations. The two series each have a different length (e.g. 7 pitches and 10 durations) so that the pattern does not repeat for many measures, if at all (i.e. the passage may be shorter than the length needed to arrive back at the original synchronization). Isorhythm can still prove fascinating to a composer as a way to construct a passage that is assured of having some continuity (because of a limited set of pitches and durations) as well as some variety and usually a degree of aural unpredictability (despite the fact that there is repetition of each series) due to the choosing of complex ratio between the two sets. An effective 20th-century example can be found in the piano part of the first movement of Messiaen's *Quartet for the End of Time*, where the passage serves as a complex background textural sonority.

I found that using a Sudoku game as the basis for a (sketch of) a compositional form can provide a nice way to introduce both mapping and the concepts of serial music to composition students.[45] Interestingly, Messiaen's pioneering foray into serialism was confined to a 9-note pitch set, which is far easier to follow structurally than with the 12-tone set that replaced it, as the ear does not become exhausted with the full set of pitches and as such is closer to a typical 7-note scale.[46]

---

45. Students were asked to assign any parameters they wish to the numbers and, optionally, empty spaces (if the Sudoku game is not completed); they then had to determine how the sudoku is 'read' to produce a musical passage.

46. See Ch. 9 for more discussion.

15. The shifting scale of consonance / dissonance

Consonance and dissonance are words that are used only occasionally outside of a musical context, in my experience. Within the music world, they are very well known in conjunction with pitch intervals, and much less known - but very handy - in talking about rhythm. It seems that there is a fairly straightforward scale (in the non-musical sense), with 'extremely consonant' on one end and 'extremely dissonant' on the other. What is sometimes not made sufficiently clear in undergraduate music courses is that the marker of dissonance shifts towards 'consonant' with time: that is, we seem to become increasingly tolerant of the harshness of a dissonance. (This seems to be true for rhythmic consonance and dissonance as well.) To confuse matters further, the notion of 'consonance' has some links with 'good' and 'harmonious', which tends to imply that dissonance is a bad thing. As we know, however, a piece with no dissonance would be quite boring. Another criterion seems linked to aesthetic preference: some of us prefer a high level of dissonance and will get bored with "too much" consonance. The same is true for complexity, and I assume the two are closely related. What hasn't been researched, to my knowledge, is to what extent one's dissonance level tolerance is the same for pitch and rhythm – but I suspect it can be different. (That is, I suspect that on a scale of 1-10, where 10 is the most dissonant possible, I appreciate a 9 in rhythm and only a 7 in pitch. But it might make an interesting study.)

There is some analogy between consonance and predictability as well. Predictability is also something that is often appreciated, but without some unpredictability, boredom is again a likely effect. Therefore, there is a close link between parsing and dissonance tolerance – which means that the familiarity of the musical style or language will greatly affect the perception. This implies that dissonance can wane (slightly) during the course of a piece – which makes intuitive sense.

It has been argued that pitch consonance is rooted in the specific relation of the intervals within the harmonic series: those which are closest to the simpler ratios (octave, perfect fifth, etc.) are more consonant. Of course, this is more difficult to grasp when dealing with equal temperament (see Ch. 9) as the intervals are no longer within those exact proportions - and to have an interval that is *almost* perfectly consonant may be perceived as more dissonant than one which is farther away, just as, within the equal-tempered system, a minor second and its inversion the major seventh are usually regarded as presenting harsher dissonances than a major second or minor seventh. A little-known exploration by the Czech theorist Janeček (not the similarly-named composer) led to his classification of chords according to their degree of consonance / dissonance. This was based on the various component intervals, and makes sense to the ear - but is not generally well-integrated into common theoretical studies.

The term 'rhythmic dissonance' was proposed initially by Joseph Schillinger and developed significantly by Yeston (1976), with crucial refinements by Krebs (1987). It refers to a very similar definition of consonance as that in pitch (Stockhausen would probably say that it is identical, just farther down the scale of periodicities). Rhythms which relate in a 1:2 or 1:3 ratio are perceived as less dissonant than more complex ones, such as 2:3 or 15:16. However, there is still work to be done on investigating the degree of dissonance presented by different contexts. It is likely that when two layers of music seem sufficiently 'segregated' (according to Auditory Scene Analysis principles) – for example by register and timbre as well as by rhythmic organization – that any rhythmic dissonance will be considered simply (and usually unconsciously) as another segregating factor. Such research also suggests that we have more tendency to listen in a linear way (what score-readers call 'horizontally') than to simultaneously-presented series of sounds ('vertical sonorities'), despite analysts' assumption of the latter. To conclude: perception of dissonance depends not only on the music and the listener's aesthetic preference and experience with the particular musical language, but also on his/her degree of focus, interest, inclination, and mood.

16. Notation as a composer's tool (or:
Transcribing the Muse)

As discussed in Ch. 19, analysis should not rely exclusively on notation. However, flawed as it may be, notation does have its functions: not only in providing directions by the composer for the performer(s) - including the conductor, if applicable – but also in helping the composer work out ideas.

Most composers who notate music for performers will go through several or many versions before they are satisfied with the finished score. It seems that many non-composers have little information about this whole process - partly because it is rarely shared, and probably because most composers don't want everyone to see their rejected or pre-polished ideas. Also, there are several different ways of proceeding, and some may seem more "acceptable" than others. Increasingly, the final product is produced in a notation software on a computer, and many probably work from start to finish with such software, though this has its own dangers.

It seems that the ideal solution for the composer would be to imagine everything in detail mentally, and then write it all down when done. However, this is quite difficult. The ideas become more 'frozen' when notated, so it becomes more challenging to change them if they are not placed down 'correctly' in the first try. By using the term 'correctly', I am implying that the best solution is in the head, and that the act of notation involves searching for the best way to write it down. This is not always the case: an idea may well change (for the better, sometimes) as it is being notated, or after one has looked at it written. But in general, the process of notation and composition and performance is a bit of a compromise between what the composer really wants and what is possible to transmit (and perform). This may be more typical of an electroacoustic composer's thinking than of a purely acoustic one – the reason some of us choose electroacoustics is to have more precise control over a greater set of elements. (It is not always the most efficient nor the most satisfying way to produce music, however; the performer can usually add not only life but also his or her own creative imagination to the process, and the electronic studio can be not only a lonely and frustrating place to work, but also full of so many sonic possibilities that one almost always becomes side-tracked when trying to produce a certain sound. Therefore, it promotes a different way of approaching the compositional process).

Assuming that one has a sonic idea in one's head, how does one determine how to notate it? It depends: on the idea, the composer, and the circumstances. If writing for a woodwind quintet, for example, then one may have ideas of what the clarinet and flute might play. But if one just has an idea of an interesting sonic gesture, then one needs to figure out what instruments could be used to produce it.

In some cases, the composer makes graphic sketches – often coloured. These may be a kind of doodling, which then have to be 'translated' into sound, or they may be sketched on a time-line (often left-to-right, like conventional Western music notation) that indicates the order in which things will happen. This is a good way of figuring out passages where more than one sonic event may coexist. In some cases, the actual duration of the events is determined only later; in other words, the time-line is not yet specified in terms of units, and might be seconds or minutes. Such sketches allow one to clarify the distinct character and texture of each component part, and convey the ways in which they might evolve over time (becoming more compact registrally, or denser, or changing timbre, or fragmenting).

Another very typical stage of working on the compositional ideas - sometimes a second phase after the graphic sketches, or a preliminary one – involves scribbling down melodic, textural, harmonic, and/or gestural fragments. These may be only a few notes long, and are sometimes only half-notated – written on score paper, for example, but without specific pitches or durations indicated, only approximations with wide-nibbed pens. After being refined into something close to specific notation, they can be sorted into categories producing piles of "textures", "gestures", "melodies", "chords". Similarities might be noticed between specific intervallic content and contours of the fragments – which will imply, if not already specified, which instruments, registers, amplitude, and tempi they are destined for. Sometimes they will be indelibly tied to only one particular profile, but sometimes they can be modified. In my more cerebral days, I would also note which fragment could occur only once or twice before losing its 'punch', and which could recur numerous times; which could lead into which other ones smoothly; which would provoke dramatic contrast, etc. Do others proceed this way? A few, probably – there are now symposia being organized to probe into compositional method, in direct and indirect ways (e.g. tied to technology).

As mentioned in previous chapters, the traditional notation systems we have inherited are quite imprecise and rather inappropriate for some perfectly sound musical ideas. To invent new notation is not the simple solution it might first seem – because one has to ensure that the performers are willing to invest the time to learn how to read it. Many do not seem to realize that performers learn muscular patterns triggered by what they see on the page – it goes far beyond an intellectual grasp of what is being asked. However, notational devices such as using a time-line rather than barlines for temporal placement are both very easy to read and very liberating for the composer, in some circumstances. And on a smaller level, indicating a fluctuation in vibrato or trill speed by an analogous fluctuation in a line above the staff is equally easy to read. Other notational additions are not so difficult to learn either – but need to be introduced earlier in the performer's training to optimize results. New trends in animated notation are also proving to be welcome for various complex contemporary performance situations, such as those involving other artforms (dance, theatre), improvisation, or digital elements.[47]

It would be gratifying to see more highly-qualified composers becoming involved with the creation of improved resources for developing performance techniques – such as études and short pieces for beginners. The usefulness of learning major and minor scales in traditional music training, for example, is because so many works from the 18th and 19th centuries contained fragments of such scalar passages. It is one of the glaring oversights of 20th-century instrumental pedagogy that these are not routinely supplemented – as they are in jazz - by octatonic scales, whole-tone arpeggios, patterns of seconds and sevenths, different-length *glissandi*, etc. Études likewise should abound in additive rhythms, timbral shifts, pitch bends, intricate amplitude curves, and alternate tunings. Mixed music, whereby a performer plays with pre-recorded or live-generated by computer sounds, is usually reserved for very advanced performers – but with the ease of sound production on computers, even many beginning students can learn to play a piece which includes a simple pre-recorded component to prepare them for more complex mixed music situations (an electroacoustic track, for example, not simply a pre-recorded backup band of the

---

47. A good overview is provided in Cat Hope's article "The Future is Graphic: animated notation for contemporary practice" Hope 2020.

'Music-Minus-One' type). And doubtless, such repertoire would help narrow the gap between the world of avant-garde experimentation and simple playable repertoire. Meanwhile, the composer who takes the time to find some willing performers to work with, and learns what is easy and what is difficult, will find that the shortcomings of notation dissolve when one can supplement them with the benefits of oral tradition that still forms the core of instrumental training.

17. Mood, emotion, character (*or:* What's expression got to do with it?)

For those outside the ivory walls of academia, it may come as a surprise to learn that there is often little talk about expression – and even emotion – in the music academy. There are two distinct reasons for this:

- an early 20th-century strategy practiced by many in humanities to imbue more "scientific" modes of study into their investigations (in an effort, no doubt, to present themselves as worthy rivals of their colleagues in the 'hard sciences', that had expanded with startling directions since the mid-19th century); *and*

- a (perhaps corresponding) shift of aesthetics on the part of many composers.

However, as much if not most music does have emotive effect on much of its audience, those who wish to focus on that need to have accepted means of doing so within scholarly discourse. What were the reasons for avoiding the subject?

i. puritanical traits: trying to suppress any display of human emotion on the grounds that it's inappropriate – a view often supported by fundamentalists in different religions and cultures: the "stiff upper lip" policy, avoiding boisterous behaviour or demonstrations of affection;

ii. embarrassment about the rather idiosyncratic descriptions of music that became popular among junior critics around the late 19th / early 20th century, whereby melodies became anthropomorphized according to the personal whims of the writer;

iii. a sense of futility due to the realization that so many people have different emotional responses to the same music;

iv. a lack of terminology for discussing emotions in

music - probably a direct result of the preceding factors (i), (ii), and (iii).

These reasons may have contributed to another phenomenon that hindered improvement throughout the 20th century: an extraordinarily high concentration of attention on cerebral aspects of music not only in 20th-century musicology but even standard undergraduate textbooks about music history.[48] This has led to a focus on those composers who enjoy(ed) concentrating on intellectual aspects, rather than those who create music more intuitively. An early example is Schoenberg: it was typical to stress his admirably strict use of tone rows rather than to what extent he was able to maintain all the traditional aspects of dramatic late 19th-century music – phrasing, dynamics, ranges, timbres, tempi, etc. – even when the natural choosing of pitch was substituted by the 12-tone system (or by *sprechgesang*, on the other end of the scale).

At the same time, Stravinsky appealed to many people who were not particularly enamoured of Schoenberg's (or late 19th-century) style. Stravinsky was one of the first really 'abstract' composers since Classical times (in music history terms, i.e. 18th century, not ancient Greece) in the sense of 'abstract art'. His early works like *The Rite of Spring* seem strikingly close to Constructivism, for example, which must have been a direct influence on him.[49] Abstract art is generally considered non-pictorial, and usually makes no

---

48. Ironically, but perhaps inevitably, some recent work in the New Musicology sphere addresses these issues – such as Queer Studies – but it is often cloaked in dense prose which may seem inscrutable to the uninitiated. It is as though the wordiness will balance out the emotion under discussion.

49. I have not yet seen this discussed in academia, but given that Constructivisim, a striking shift in sculpture, was pioneered by Russian sculptors with links to Paris, it seems unlikely that it was unknown to him.

obvious reference to human (or any other organic) form.

Systems of compositional organization are relatively easy to talk about: it may take months to decode a piece, but this is a very useful way to spend one's time if one wishes to feel one is working hard, without having to confront messy issues like emotional content. And many composers are fascinated with numbers and systems – perhaps in the same way that some autistic children are. The love of music that is strong enough to lead someone to devote her/his life to creating it has often been said to go along with a predilection for mathematics. So, there are probably many composers and musicologists who find this bias perfectly reasonable.

Now there is another factor that comes into play: academic degrees and exams. Pieces and compositional styles whose attributes are easy to identify ("see the cleverness of this structure underlying Stockhausen's work?") became much more talked about – and gradually those works whose potency could not be so easily explained were discarded. Similarly, creative artists who were not inclined to work within such bounds did not feel part of the 'current scene' and often wandered into other less-defined areas (like free jazz).

Oddly enough, it seems that the music psychologists have been more assiduous in pursuing this line of enquiry more than musicologists, although that is now changing. For one reason, they are more concerned with the impact of music on non-musicians - as it has been found useful in health contexts as well as more questionable areas like advertising. However, researchers like John Sloboda (see for ex. Juslin & Sloboda 2001) have helped bring this topic more openly into musicological circles.

SECTION III:

TRANSMISSION FROM CREATOR TO LISTENER / CRITIC

The remaining sections (III-V) of this book discuss other topics that are not exclusive to music (communication, cognition, acoustic ecology) but that greatly influence (or should influence) musicological research. Again, these are topics that are often neglected in a musician's education, and their inclusion here is due to my belief that they should be incorporated into the training of Conversational Musicologists - if not all musicians. Due to the absence of many of these topics from traditional academic discourse, I have been obliged to write in even more subjective and casual style than usual, as the framework and language for such discussion is not obvious to me.

18. Transmission paths & carriers of the music (or: Performers, technological wizardry, critical analysts, & the vagaries of human reception mechanisms)

Many years ago, I bought a CD of music by women composers: Clara Schumann, Amy Beach, someone else... and was quite disappointed (and embarrassed, as a fellow woman composer) upon listening. It was years later that I realized, on retrieving it from a box in a dark corner, that it was not the music itself that was weak, but both the performance and the recording quality. Given that this was the reaction of someone eager to hear fresh approaches to composition, one can guess the reaction of the many people who have already been led to believe that music by women composers are generally weaker (reinforced by excluding people like Bacewicz from the standard history books).

The qualities that make a dynamic performance so much better than a lack-luster one are often in the precise realm where our vocabulary is lacking. Performance in particular is difficult to judge without an intimate knowledge of the composer's intention – assuming that composer and performer are not the same person. (There are also instances where a composer gives a weak performance of her/his own work, due to a lack of sufficient performance skills unrelated to their skill as composers.)

In the traditional Western model, there is a transmission path from composer to audience that depends on the intervention of the performer(s) and the specific acoustic space and instrument characteristics. Nowadays, even in the realm of purely acoustic performance, the recording process (engineer plus quality of recording and playback equipment) is also affecting the path dramatically.

There are several human factors that affect the quality of the transmission signal and therefore dependent on both performer and receptor: e.g. conviction, effort, concentration, and sincerity level, along with others that we might classify as 'intelligence' and 'health'. Intelligence relates in part to the speed at which things can be conceptually grasped, efficiently stored, retrieved quickly at appropriate times, and applied. The concept of health has to do both with the health and sensitivity of the sense organs that receive the various information (see Ch. 23 on information retrieval) and the overall state of the entire organism, including lack of stress (from factors such as noise, information overload, caffeine levels, etc.) which will allow the intellect and the intuitive sides to work together in counterpoint, if not harmony, to interpret what is received.

Another factor in the clarity of communication is the degree of 'articulateness'. Imagine what we mean when we talk about an "articulate speaker" in a detailed physical sense, such as a speaker who doesn't mumble, and thus the individual words can be easily comprehended. The musical term of articulation, which refers broadly to a set of performance technique conventions, seems to work in direct analogy to human speech - more overtly with wind instruments - such as "crisp articulation" or "slurred". However, the concept is equally relevant in the broader terms of language, as when we refer to a particularly articulate researcher. This presumably means that the person has not only made excellent choices of words and analogies to express her/himself, but also that s/he has well-organized thoughts and knows what s/he is wishing to say.

It is in this sense of "articulate" that more attention could be directed in music. The performers' ability to articulate clearly is critically dependent on their technique, but also on their understanding of the composer's intent. Therefore, it relates both to the ability to 'parse' what is found in the music (for example, seen in the score, through some form of analysis) and the ability to transfer it effectively ("musically") to the listener(s). Of course, this assumes that the composer is also sufficiently articulate to make his or her intent clear. For a composer, being articulate involves developing an idea and recognizing its essential characteristics (desired character of aural imagery, behaviour, environment) *and* having the skills to notate it effectively enough - if necessary - to be deciphered by a competent performer / ensemble – or to create it in the computer / electronic studio (or both). It is often difficult for the listener, whether an inexperienced musician or a non-musician, to identify the culprits - composer, performers, acoustics, other factors, or a combination of all - in a lack-lustre performance.

Somewhere affecting this transmission is the concept of marketing. In its broadest sense, marketing will affect our reception of the piece due to our opinion of the composer, the performer, the venue, the genre, the recording label, etc. – and all of these are liable to intense market pressure. In the past, there used to be two other roles in the transmission path: a chooser and a describer. By 'chooser' I mean the person or persons responsible for choosing a certain work for a concert (or recording), such as the organizer or patron. The describer was often some type of musicologist or critic, who would explain the work or at least the style or genre and what we should be listening for. This would not have to be someone present at the concert, but simply someone like a critic - or a professor, or companion - who urged people to listen to that composer's work and to appreciate their particular attention to one or another aspect: exquisite harmonies, well-crafted melodies, bold use of dissonance, etc.

Even if one feels skeptical about the critics' opinions of a certain performer and confident that one can ignore them - or generally shies away from hype - one can easily fall under the sway of conventions. For example, many feel that a good orchestral piece, for example, should be more than 7 minutes long and not more than 45, and fully expect that the violins should play for a good percentage of the work's duration. In addition, it now seems standard practice to assume that any really good work will become recognized as such by a wide body of people. Although eminently reasonable – as it is arguable that a musical work needs to be able to communicate something to someone - the required time-span for a contemporary work to become recognized as significant seems to have shrunk from a century or so to a year or two, whereas the number of people who have to participate in the approval has swollen to an indiscriminate number, regardless of their qualifications as critical listeners. If marketing is so influential, why do more of us not engage in it more? As mentioned elsewhere, certain upbringings often encourage a modesty that is incompatible with the kind of insistent brashness that seems to be equated with persuading people to listen – so why do we not collectively campaign for some new preferences – from diversity in concert hall seating conventions to diversity in 'acceptable' durations of pieces and diversity in the sound: silence ratio?

19. Notation for the analyst (or: The reluctance to trust one's hearing)

Not all good music is notated – and even when the music is notated, those dots and lines do not reveal all the important information. In fact, 'standard' notation is inadequate for transmitting many of the subtleties of pitch, rhythm, and timbre that today's composer wishes to incorporate. As a result, past and current analytical practice that demonstrates an over-dependence on the written score is weak. Any good musicologist knows that the music has to be heard in one's own head while analyzing.

Although written notation can be an extremely efficient way of determining many aspects of the music's structure, such as harmonic progressions, it can also be misleading or simply absent. Notation grew out of a type of mnemonics, a set of instructions to the performer who already had an internal idea of what would be produced - whether because he or she had previously invented it, or learned it from someone else. Gradually the notation conventions became sufficiently sophisticated that a composer could treat the notation as a set of instructions to a performer who could learn it without 'human intervention'. However, the performer had almost always studied with another individual in order to learn how such manuscripts should be decoded. In other words, the performance of traditional styles became a style of 'oral tradition'.

With the advent of the twentieth century, a proliferation of styles (and in some cases, the crossing of one style with another) created problems with score interpretation. As composers explored new forms and techniques, they wished to expand the vocabulary on such elements as timbre and rhythm. As a result, assumptions on aspects that referred to desired timbral shape and phrasing became eroded. Some composers tried to overcome this through increasingly detailed instructions, but as a result many performers were overwhelmed and retreated into the music of earlier times – or different genres. The problem was that such details had never had to be articulated before, having been transmitted by oral tradition. Words and/or diagrams could often convey a sense of what was needed, but the time required to puzzle out a phrase was often greatly magnified, and the time lapse between first seeing a score and being able to bring it into audible reality increased sufficiently to discourage all but the hardiest and most curious.[50] It is also not clear that being able to hear a MIDI rendition of an unperformed score is actually helpful, as it is worse than a lacklustre performance (see Ch. 18).

A few pioneering composers, including Steve Reich and Pauline Oliveros, counter-responded to this situation by assembling small groups of performers (often other composers) with whom they would work over a period of months or years, thereby incorporating the oral with the written tradition again. Another response, that of incorporating improvisation, was adopted by many composers to varying degrees. This gave the performers more of their former role whereby their own expertise authorized their individual contributions to the score's instructions. Some of the more extreme examples of this are found in process works. At the other extreme were composers who simply introduced some elasticity through a reverting to traditional terms such as *ad lib.* and *con rubato*.

Probably the clearest example of the dominance of

---

50. There are also instances where a composer gives a weak performance of her/his own work, because they are amateur performers – or at least not sufficiently skilled to play extremely difficult work - even if they are expert composers – as well as the converse.

notation on analysis has been felt by the electroacoustic community (by which I include computer music, electronic music, music for live performers and fixed media, etc.). In many cases, this music has no score at all. When scores do exist, they may be partial, as in works for mixed live and tape. In cases where there is some type of notation, it may not be of the traditional type of instructions to the performer, but simply a graphic representation that allows the live musicians involved to identify cues in pre-recorded tracks - and allows the analyst to have a visual representation to point to. When a score does take the form of instructions, it may be arcane instructions to a laptop user which demand knowledge of a particular software or specific patch being used.

If there is no score, then the analyst has the choice of (a) ignoring the work - which seems to have been the overwhelming tendency in the last sixty years - or (b) looking for alternative methodologies. In the electroacoustic world, considerable progress has been made in inventing and developing tools and strategies for notating the audio result of a work in meaningful or at least relevant ways. [51] These may incorporate text, graphics, and sound; and although not all are designed to reveal elements of more traditional forms (such as harmony), a creative analyst can always blend different analytical approaches into a hybrid. Graphics often incorporate amplitude and/or spectral graphs that give most users a sense of being a viable record, because it is a recording of the actual sonic signal.

Of course, those who are aware of psychology, information transmission, and other factors realize that such charts can be misleading as well as incomprehensible; for example, the listener's sense of time may not coincide with a strict clock time, although it serves as an equally viable measure. Likewise, our ability to distinguish different signals

---

51. See for example assorted articles in the journal *Organised Sound*.

from a soundscape is perhaps one of the most impressive capacities of human cognition, and the fields of auditory scene analysis (see Ch. 23) and music information retrieval (Ch. 28) have both been working towards development of cognitive models to explain this feat. Until now, there are very inadequate representations of our hearing that can be taught to a computer to turn a complex sonic signal into something resembling our own hearing of it.

It seems imperative to focus more research energy into an attention to auditive analysis, in order to complement traditional score analysis and to be able to analyze works that include improvisation, pre-recorded signals, or other sounds that may not be clearly indicated by a score (such as live processing of a performer's signal). If one decides to tackle auditive analysis, though, there are other issues that need to be addressed: what audio signal is being analyzed? In simple terms, there are several options: a single performance, a single recording of a performance, or multiple versions of either or both. In all of these cases, it makes sense to reflect on the performance itself, where the acoustic conditions blur into the socio-cultural ones: is the sound clearly heard? is it important to the audience that it be clearly heard? And from here, it is equally valid to move into the more philosophical questions: is there an audience? is an audience necessary to validate it? Are all the performances approximations of the 'ideal' that can only be imagined? etc.

It is interesting to consider this concept of the 'ideal' performance that one might hear in one's head. Do all real performances fall short of a single 'ideal', or can there be various equally dynamic representations? As mentioned earlier, many aspects of a performance are scarcely visible in a score – from nuances of pitch and amplitude to shifts of timbre due to combinations of amplitude, articulation, register, and instrumentation. Therefore, a performer needs to provide some degree of interpretation, and thus may provide an 'enhanced' version that is not identical to what the composer had originally imagined.

In many cases, these questions are not so relevant: the analyst can find a preferred performance or two, and replay them from a recording until basically memorized. However, in the case of contemporary music – and in early music that has not been sustained through oral tradition in the intervening centuries - the piece may never have been played, or may well have been played 'imperfectly'. After all, most great performances imply a good analysis first – this analysis may well be done on an intuitive level by the performer, but most good performers will have some background in analysis from their basic training, and that analysis course usually involved works by analysts. So, with contemporary works, the musical language may need some 'unravelling' or study before any performer can fully grasp how it could best be interpreted. Except in very rare cases where one is examining a composer's notational style, or examining the dynamics of live performance, I tend to agree with those who think that it is the imagined performance that should be the focus of any analysis.

This leads to another related topic, concerning the development of a sophisticated aural imagination. Hearing an imaginary performance on viewing a score was admittedly easier to do when the options were more limited – e.g. a 19th-century composition student who was familiar with studying a score with regular meter and predictable harmonies before and after hearing it, and many others in the same genre, performed live. Analysts who can hear complex 20th / 21st century musical works in their heads are often those who have participated in similar works as performers, and so they also have highly-developed senses of the correspondence between score and resultant sound. However, many younger students have much more difficulty because of an over-reliance on computer software that allows them to have an instant – but distorted - playback of a musical passage.

Once one has become comfortable with the need for auditive analysis, and especially once one has contemplated the issues of performance in general, it is difficult to regard a score from the 18th or 19th century without reflecting on this larger context. As mentioned, it can be supposed that a mere century ago, the analyst who was studying a score was usually hearing it in his or her mind, as the styles of performance were fewer and more familiar. In addition, the analyst's main acquaintance with any music was usually through live performance. For this reason, the emphasis on the written notation was not as heavy as might appear from looking at their analyses; everyone was assumed to be hearing the works in their heads as they looked at the written symbols on the page. However, many analyses being submitted these days by music students, even at the graduate level, are not based on such a clear audio signal. Not only are many of the more recent scores referring to extremely complex sonorities, but the knowledge of the sound of instruments is often second-hand, often deliberately altered - sometimes quite substantially - by sound engineers who believe that they can improve the work by acoustical 'shading'. To make matters worse, the recordings may be listened to on inferior speakers and by ears that have been damaged by urban soundscapes if not dangerous decibel levels at concerts.

Another contributing factor to the possible mis-interpretation of written scores is the prevalence of notation software. Though seductive in some aspects, they are quite capable of destroying the young musician's aural imagination, as a note (or passage, or full composition) can be written and played back to check whether it is the right one, rather than being imagined and then notated.

The confusing of the aural signal of a MIDI violin with a live one may seem impossible for those of us who are used to live music (and violins), but it is a phenomenon that can be witnessed in many students. Listening to a MIDI version can be quite deceptive: microscopic detail of pitch, timbre, dynamics, and tempo are often omitted, so that a slow-moving passage may sound wonderful on acoustic instruments, but tediously banal in MIDI. It is rather like looking at a poor-quality black-&-white photocopy of a photograph of a painting to determine whether one wants to buy the original.

20. Confusing interface with content (or: Differences and commonalities of computer music, techno, sound effects, symphonies)

The various sub-fields of electroacoustic music (see Appendix B) tend to have their own venues and audiences due in large part to technological requirements – but many characteristics of the 'genre', as it is sometimes regarded, may be shared by other compositional styles. To a first-time listener, the aesthetics may seem quite different between a concert of fully invisible sound sources in a large and dark room and the performance of costumed humans on stage producing sounds through visible physical movements. However, composers who have worked with or been influenced by electroacoustics may transfer their concepts of sound into the acoustic realm, and occasionally one hears quite traditional pitch-based works with rich acoustic-instrument-type timbres produced digitally with a hint of physical gestures.

In an early 20th-century encyclopedia entry on film music, a well-known musicologist scoffs at those who create realistic correspondences between sound and image, on the grounds that anyone can create sound effects (if only!) but these cannot be considered true art. This is reminiscent of the early electroacoustics opinion (still prevalent in some places) that one should never try to produce a sound that resembles an existing instrument. The original motivation for this attitude in electroacoustics contexts was doubtless meant simply to promote more creative exploration – but it seems extremely restrictive, and to a large degree responsible for the alienation of many audiences, as it removes potential threads of recognition that can balance other less familiar elements in a work (such as formal concerns or timbral extensions). The idea of the comment is probably linked to focussing on the poetic or artistic (or poietic) rather than on the realistic. However, it seems to me that learning to (re-)create a realistic effect could easily be considered a very useful part of one's training: it has the benefit of being easily 'testable' by both the practitioner and his/her teachers/friends. There are two parallels in the visual arts world: (i) the training of a drawer or painter often relies on a hefty amount of 'life drawing', still life, etc. in order to ensure that one is capable of creating any given desired impression, including organic and emotive qualities; and (ii) the European tradition often includes a copying of other artists' works as an important step in training (at a size other than the original, to avoid forgeries). In music, this second step is still maintained in some European music traditions, through the composing of pieces in the style of Haydn or Schumann, for example, and taught in a separate course (called in French for example "techniques d'écriture" as distinguished from the personally creative "composition livre").

The study of how to create vocal-like sounds with computers is an interesting case in point; this was conducted notably by Bell Labs – looking for a way to save money by getting rid of telephone operators around the land – and therefore clearly in the realm of science, not art. But due to a few particular and unique individuals such as Max Mathews, John Chowning, and Jean-Claude Risset, the research flowed straight into art and was enhanced by artistic perspectives. There were many others who worked hard on creating computer sounds to resemble instruments (for synthesizers, etc.) which were then used, normally by other people, to create music without having to employ full studio orchestras. (Perhaps this was another motivation for the "prohibition" on creating instrument-like sounds – to ward off potential criticism that the electroacoustic gang were threatening the livelihood of performers.)

When one looks at music through the lens of auditory perception research, one begins to realize that acoustic instruments were usually refined to be particularly appealing – and that appeal would relate to our own accuracy of frequency differentiation around the human speech range, for example, as well as other properties that could affect our sense of perceiving the instrument, or a particular ensemble of instruments, as appearing clearly identifiable to our sensory awareness. For example, the voice-like qualities of certain instruments – from kamancheh to english horn – give those instruments very expressive potential.

A more modern issue emerges when a sonic representation makes an effort to be 'faithful' – as in a photograph or a recording – but the technology itself is incapable of producing a fully realistic image. When we listen to early recordings of Caruso, for example, we can hear artefacts of the recording itself (which in time adds a kind of patina, like the discoloured varnish on paintings of the 'Early Masters'); or when we see a photograph, it may be not only less sharply focussed but also in grayscale. There has been a recent attempt to remedy these technological shortcomings that appears to me like quite a desperate search for increasingly high resolution that rather misses the point. Images of nature scenes on high-resolution television screens can appear quite unrealistic to those of us who have less-than-perfect vision in real life. When hiking in the mountains, we don't perceive things with that level of detail at every depth, and with a glassy sheen. Moreover, when we move a bit to left or right in front of the screen, the image shifts in a way that never quite lines up with the camera-person's movements (who is generally a different size and shape). Also, as anyone who attended a 60s 'happening' knows, documenting is rarely ideal: 'you had to be there'. For such happenings, not only was there a lack of high-resolution colour video cameras to pick up multiple angles of the scene, but there was no way of transmitting the full sensorial environment and its 'vibes'.

This issue is now compounded by another problem. These days, there are many people who have absolutely no mental image of the sound production when they listen to recorded music, as they have not been to live concerts or even watched someone practicing. Given the increasing amount of pseudo-instruments and audio engineering, even with good quality recording and playback it is becoming increasingly rare to listen to a 'straight' recording of a live performance. If the speakers are the embedded ones on the laptop computer or a cheap set of headphones with street noises only partially blocked out, the problem is compounded. No recording is 'invisible', but those of us with years of listening to live concerts can recognize some as being considerably more life-like; our imaginations allow us to build on what we hear, to reconstruct the image we want.

21. Post-colonial ears and the search for the exotic

A receptiveness to different musical ideas seems to me a natural characteristic of an artistic temperament – and in fact for many years I assumed that a 'true' artist would always have a full-blown curiosity for art from other cultures and time periods (along with a passion to experience diverse natural environments) as potential fodder for his or her own creative ideas. However, this seems a biased view encouraged by a Western European / North American mid-20th century stance, heightened in my case by extensive travel and hob-nobbing with others who did the same. In fact, the degree of experimentation with traditional styles – aesthetics, forms, tunings, instrumentation - can remain very slight in some cultural environments for millennia: hence the fairly clear demarcation - until a century ago - between music of different regions. So an artist can think that she or he is being very inventive without ever leaving what appears from a foreign perspective as a narrow range of possibilities.

But there has clearly been transmission between different musical cultures over the ages. A study of organology traces the influence of instruments – the claim of Persian ancestry (santur) for the Chinese guqin and Japanese koto, for example – that leads me to reflect that in fact a single minstrel could be responsible for bringing a catchy tune from one part of the world to another, and performing it well enough for it to become included in the local repertoire. Imagine then the potential effect of six hundred years of court music in Moorish Iberia, with skilled musicians from Baghdad and elsewhere in the Arabic and Persian worlds, on the development of European Renaissance music.

110

A general fascination with the exotic seems to go in waves, and that of the late 19th century Europe, as characterized by the Paris 1889 Exposition, is often mentioned in music texts as providing exposure of foreign music (such as Indonesian gamelan) to local composers (such as Debussy). To many visitors, this must have been a mere curiosity in the manner of the human zoo also present. But to Debussy, his fascination with the sounds and formal aspects were incorporated into his own creative practice. What happens in such cases is always tempered by the "home" culture – and the composer's own culturally-derived filters, such as the easily-believable story that the "gypsies" from whom Brahms learned much of his source material for the Hungarian Dances were in fact music students, adapting local tunes to their restaurant gigs.

Some conservatism may be dictated by government or religious practice – and, as the audiences became bigger, by popular trends. Nowadays we have more subtle influences such as notation software that gives clear preference to certain styles, and digital instruments that favour a single tuning system. However, on the whole, the latter part of the 20th century has seen a real explosion of contact with other cultures and simultaneously the proliferation of audiences for any particular musical style. Finally, we are hearing a proliferation of convincing fusions between cultures, moving beyond pastiches and incoherent pairings of disparate styles to truly new forms and languages. When two or more musicians from different cultures meet, oral tradition can allow for a rich exchange of stylistic detail, and now such exchanges can be enhanced by recording technologies and telematics to allow for a potentially more accelerated pace of acquisition and cross-regional transfer.

The question is: how much of the lure of the exotic depends on the sound appearing "foreign" and how long before its exoticism evaporates?

22. When sound is art but not music; when music is sound but not art (soundscape, film music, installation art, performance art, sound effects, ringtones...)

We have very good analytical methods for some types and styles of music. But there has been a tendency in 'classical (Western European) musicology' to treat certain styles only to be worthy of study. It could be that this was not the fault of the original scholars – who just happened to be curious about those particular styles – but eventually it became assumed, with a little bit of help from those who were benefitting from the status quo, that the types of music studied were the only ones worth treating seriously. Thus we have music professors who explain to the class that Prokofieff's music for films was inferior to his purely acoustic works, and excused him for having stooped so low on the grounds that 'he probably needed the money'. Likewise, in the discussions of works like *The Rite of Spring* during a history class, it is always mentioned that it was written for ballet - but analyses rarely seemed to take that into consideration. Surely the movements of the dancers - both individual limb and full body movement, and the collective movements of the troupe or a sub-group - would have a huge impact on both the receiver and the composer designing it.

To some extent, this bias against non-concert music derives simply from a lack of cross-disciplinary conversation, with the resulting paucity of terminology and even conceptual frameworks (or vice-versa). Then, because we lack the necessary language and analytical tools, we can't actually say much about the quality of the film music, especially in comparison to non-film music.

Why could one not however discuss two different works for film by Prokofieff and compare them to each other, for example? Presumably that could be useful, and perhaps provide some insight into film music composing because it is someone we 'know' from other contexts. And even more logically, why are more composition students not encouraged, or even mandated, to compose at least one work for a short dance, act from a play, figure skating routine, or art installation as part of their training?

The slow development of appropriate tools for multimedia analysis in particular was doubtless impacted by the technological difficulties, until the last decade or so, of sharing audio-visual material. Imagine the difficulty of specifying within a written article, perhaps with some black & white line drawings, how a musical passage enhances, underscores, counterpoints, or negates the mood of a particular dance segment to readers who have had no opportunity to view the dance in question. Finally, collections of scholars are emerging who are both technology-literate and interested in musicology. It is no coincidence that some of the most appropriate software tools (such as Couprie's *EAnalysis* and *iAnalyse*, and the *Acousmographe* from GRM) were invented by those with a close knowledge of electroacoustics, because they had a higher percentage of computer-literate colleagues willing to try it out, and who were already familiar with component parts of the study such as amplitude graphs and sonograms. More conceptual bases for analysis are being developed through the emergence of new sub-disciplines. In addition, recent research in perception is starting to tackle the multimodal integration of our perception - a field which it seems could benefit from more input from musicians working in multimedia contexts.

We still struggle, however, with much that lies on the boundaries of our field. Or, perhaps they are not always on the boundaries, but in the cracks, or underground. There is a lot out there which non-musicians think of as 'music' but those of us in academia don't deign to consider: think of a continuum with cell-phone ring tones at one end, and moving through music used in advertisements, webpages, piped-in music in restaurants, bars, shopping malls, hotels. At what point do we differentiate between utilitarian sound effects and music that we may hear on some radio station inadvertently, but never consciously opt for?

Then there is the other stuff that is clearly art – performance art, or theatre, or art installations, or experimental dance, perhaps with sensors – in which there is a sonic component, but one where we do not sense the flow of music in the same way. This is truly multimedia work, but if it seems difficult to segregate the sound from the other aspects, we feel that it is not the same as music (quite right) and therefore that it is not our field (quite possibly wrong). The result is that we have lost our voice in most of the discussion about these areas.

A good start can be achieved by discussing multimedia works with people from the different disciplines involved. Temporality in art has been an essential part of music training, as in theatre and dance – but most of the performers (dancers, instrumentalists, actors) and technicians (costume and lighting designers, recording engineers, etc.) will focus mainly on the sequential linear unfolding. The composers and playwrights and choreographers need to think about form, large-scale and psychological time as well, to keep a dynamic pace, emphasize contrast, or whatever other aspects come into play. (There is some commonality with dramaturgy, but it is a term less familiar to musicians than to actors - and not the same as that used by sociologists.) For most visual artists and architects, on the other hand, temporal elements were for many centuries either ignored (a static design), or frozen like a snapshot (a sculpture of a leaping bull, a portrait or landscape). Occasionally some form of kinetic sculpture was created, and with the advent of technology like steam and electricity, these became more complex. With the coming of film, artists like Man Ray became very inventive, but decades later, many novices in painting or sculpture who decide to incorporate sounds into an installation had very little awareness of the passing of time and the factors that affect its perception.

Similarly, many beginning filmmakers have little sense of the soundtrack - or how to describe what they want to a composer. On the other hand, the art of Foley, or the creation of sound effects to accompany an image, can be a creative skill that is beyond the reach of many composers. Most of the successes seem to be left up to intuition and experimentation. With decades of sloppy pairings of clichéd orchestral writing and unconvincing acting of tired scenarios that typifies Hollywood blockbusters, we have sunk into a morass of poor-quality sound-image pairings without a loud enough clamour from those of us who can distinguish between better and worse film tracks and effects. More training in schools to match real pairings of sound and image (e.g. four slamming doors made of different materials in different spaces) would help as a first step; then an increase of critical discussion of more 'artistic' pairings. Instead, a century of disjunct sounds and images (starting with the removal of all sounds from the original footage and subsequent recording in the studio) has hindered the development of discriminating ears. Modern technology has made such possibilities easily feasible, but as yet they are not often integrated, partly because we segregate the senses by having "music" and "art" and "language" in mutually-exclusive time-slots in our training.

Early post-silent film was considered by several of its practitioners to be full of rich potential – but a potential hardly exploited. For example, Eisenstein was one of the first to argue that it would be a waste of film's potential to have the sound and the image describing the same thing. This seems parallel to the avoidance of realism in electroacoustics, with the same arguments against, at least for training purposes.

We as humans are obviously very accustomed to representation – as can be seen in cave paintings from prehistoric times. A line drawing of a running stag is obviously easy for us to grasp, despite the lack of representation of colour, detail (fur, etc.), environment (trees, etc.), as well as movement. When we come to more modern art, the choice of represented detail is often more challenging – thus, the stag could be represented by horns and fur, but without a profile. As such, though, the sense of movement (and even life) becomes easily lost. So, there is some necessity to choose the essential elements with care if the point is to conjure up the entity of the thing depicted.

There is another issue relating to the fidelity of a sound resembling an accompanying image, and vice versa; this has to do with technology, in two ways. 'Visual music' is a term that is gaining more currency,[52] although it is by no means a clear definition. Initially, it was restricted to the music-like rhythmic pacing of abstract images. However, it is now sometimes applied to abstract films where there is a soundtrack that provides a counterpoint to the rhythmic flow of the images. There are some very engaging examples, although it should be noted that highly-trained musicians are more likely to hear the results in a different way than, for example, highly-trained visual artists, as we each hear our own preferred media in a more heightened way, and therefore the counterpoint will be slightly skewed for the different participants.

---

52. Thanks in part to conferences organized by Ricardo Dal Farra and colleagues.

Michel Chion (for ex. Chion 1990) provided some ground-breaking work in organizing the several ways in which the relationship between sound and moving image can be structured:

- degree of synchronization (synchronized / lag / inexistent);

- degree of empathy (empathetic / anempathetic);

- degree of realism (hyper-realistic / realistic / unrealistic).

A short video by Alain Pelletier and Marcelle Deschênes, *Die Dyer,* struck me as a good illustration of this array of relationships. Not only are most of the possibilities demonstrated, but also the sense of 'lag' is expanded from a simple delay of sound to image (or *vice versa*) to sounds that are introduced before the image seems to match; or a sound that continues after the image changes.

Another crucial point is that our perception of sonic images is heavily influenced by our knowledge of sound-image pairings in the environment. Outside the realm of art, we expect all sounds to have a physical source – whether a human, a bird, a river, or a machine. Therefore, we doubtless have latent associations with sonic gestures and sonic imagery in music.[53]

As the creation of experiments in sound-image pairing become easier, due to technology, two main hindrances seem to fall into the realm of conversation and attitudes: either the composer has to create her/his own images, or the artist has to create his/her own sounds, or each has to find a willing and qualified collaborator. In the first case, the idea that a composer can create viable images irritates many, especially within the visual arts fields, while the same scepticism greets the visual artist who dabbles in sound (see Ch. 3). Of course, sometimes this scepticism

---

53. This is discussed further in Godøy 1997 and Mountain 2001.

is quite justified. But in order to collaborate, one needs not only willingness but also compatible strategies and vocabularies – which requires some work. One preliminary step is to establish banks of evocative sounds and images to be made available to anyone wishing to experiment, and banks of useful terms.[54]

---

54. The IMP-NESTAR project was conceived for this purpose – see Appendix D.

SECTION IV:

TRANSMISSION AMONG SCHOLARS & ARTISTS

23. How a crash course in perception & cognition can simplify everything else

My doctoral research was motivated by the conviction that analytical tools should reveal the most entrancing aspects of a work. Thus, I was shocked to realize that I could not, as a young composer, easily emulate the structures of complex works like Stravinsky's *Rite of Spring* and Messiaen's *Turangalîla* because I could not find analyses that clarified what I liked most about them: the fascinating juxtaposition and superposition of complex passages (or what I call a 'counterpoint of strata'). As many of the key elements seemed to be rhythmic, I began paying more attention to aural analysis and perceptual tendencies, as I realized that conventional Western notation is not very clear on anything rhythmic beyond a low-level structure based on duration. This led to a decade's immersion in music psychology books, journals, and conferences. Eventually, it seemed simply *inefficient* to teach any music course - whether composition, analysis, 20th-century history, or electroacoustics - without a couple of classes on auditory perception issues, memory, and information theory. For one thing, certain configurations that may appear interesting to the composer working in the abstract are in fact difficult or impossible to recognize by the listener. And in today's environment, it seems that music students need to be reassured that they should trust their ears, and then given some strategies for being able to conceptualize and transmit their aural experience.

MEMORY, INFORMATION THEORY, PARSING: It is not necessary to know much detail about memory and information theory to reach a level of understanding that will help immensely in composing and analysis. Knowing the approximate limits of echoic [<2"], short- [<6"-10"],

120

medium-, and long-term memory is enough to prompt many budding composers to see if those limits can be stretched – and some of us speculate that an attentive and exceptionally well-trained listener can stretch the short-term memory duration if given the right musical conditions.[55]

The information theory essentials can likewise be summed up very briefly: we can retain only a very limited number of "bits" of information within the short-term memory, and therefore the whole process of parsing becomes crucial even in terms of a single musical phrase. If we do not select the right 'bits', then we may not be able to recognize the appearance of a key element, and therefore not recognize its return later in the piece.

Parsing is a term borrowed from linguistic research, where it refers to the strategies used by a reader or listener to group words (e.g. into sub-phrases) in order to make sense of the sentence. In music, it refers to the way in which the listener will grasp that a certain set of notes are grouped into a melody, and that some other notes heard concurrently are to be considered as accompaniment. As with language, this is usually done subconsciously, and is considerably better for one's 'native language' than for foreign languages. The idea of a 'foreign language' is easily mapped in music onto styles and genres with which we are less familiar - and thus the arguments for early exposure to a variety of articulate musical styles are the same as those that advocate early second- (and third-) language teaching and exposure to other cultural perspectives.

The amount of time required to process all the important new elements in a piece of music is usually carefully paced by the insertion of less critical information that can be easily grasped – predictable patterns, pauses on certain notes and chords that provide the musical equivalent of

---

55. See Kramer, 1988: 371.

"redundancy" in language. (A nice, if dated, analogy on information processing is that of the telegram: the telegram had little or no redundancy, in order to save costs, and therefore usually required some reflection to understand its pithy meaning; a normal letter, however, would more closely resemble a conversation in which the meaning of a paragraph would be grasped immediately on seeing/hearing the final words.)

Thinking about what could make a 'bit' of information is itself a nice topic for reflection, and some simple examples can provide a starting point:

- a frequency;
- a collection of frequencies that seem connected by harmonic structure and behaviour [e.g. a note];
- a collection of notes that seem connected by harmonic structure & timbre [e.g. a chord, an arpeggio, a gesture, a melodic fragment];
- a collection of chords, scales, and/or arpeggios that seem connected by timbre, gesture, etc. [e.g. a phrase]; *etc.*

This explains why a trained listener (self-taught or instructed) will have quite a different appreciation of a complex piece; the information will be processed more efficiently so that larger-scale structures may become more apparent. Conversely, the high redundancy of pop music and other such genres may be void of stimulation for the same listener.

Closely related to parsing is the use of rhythmic structures: the 'clocks' provided by the beats and metric hierarchies (if present), and the subsequent changes in these structures, whether gradual or abrupt. (The use of abrupt contrast is a very strong indicator of section change, especially if used in several parameters simultaneously.)

STRATA ANALYSIS: Strata analysis refers to an analytical approach I have developed to examine those complex musical works and passages that give the effect of multiple musical ideas happening simultaneously, as though we are listening to a three-ringed circus or standing in the hallway of a conservatory listening to several students practicing independently in different rooms. Many 20th-century compositions appear to present this illusion of different coexisting layers of musical activity; it seems to be linked to an aesthetic stance that celebrates multiplicity; and is reminiscent of the definition of chaos as 'multiple orders running simultaneously'. (See Arnheim 1971) Auditory scene analysis (see Ch. 23 & Bregman 1993) is indispensable to demonstrate how the composer achieves and manipulates these illusions; concepts reminiscent of Gestalt theory such as spatial and temporal proximity are exceedingly relevant in music perception.[56]

---

56. Strata analysis is to be the subject of another future book; the basic aspects have formed the core of some special topics analysis courses and have been presented informally to colleagues. The kernels of the idea are presented, if inarticulately, in my Ph.D. dissertation, available online from my website <www.armchair-researcher.com>.

24. Music and language (*or:* The usefulness and dangers of analogies)

I have often shuddered at the quote "Music is the universal language of mankind" but only recently learned that (a) it was uttered by the poet Longfellow, and (b) there is a second half of the quote: "...and poetry their universal pastime and delight". These discoveries calmed me, because it downgraded the comment from being a belief shared by a centuries-old cultural traditions to what sounds suspiciously like an off-the cuff remark of an artist enjoying spirited conversation with friends over drinks. (The fact that he referred to "mankind" in the third person is another argument in favour of such an interpretation.) But the popularity of the saying still irritates me because it interferes with a deeper reflection on the shared domains of language and music. Although the analogy of language is quite thought-provoking, the parallels between music and language seem ill-defined, and moreover, many characteristic attributes of music are not adequately addressed by the concept.

There is a similar reflection that should also form part of introductory thinking about music composition and performance, which is: To what extent is (this) music a form of communication (and between whom?). At times music can be something else, by intention: an experiment, an exploration, an activity....

Preceding an examination of each individual term in the phrase "music is the universal language", we need to question whether or not the idea of language is being presented as a metaphor, and although I assume that this is the most common interpretation, it is possible to use the term 'language' on a meta-level, as revealed by some textbook definitions. This is a crucial distinction, as many of the difficulties of the metaphor relate to attempts to find parallels with syllables, syntax, etc. However, in this broader sense, the saying does not bear close scrutiny: surely representational sculptures and paintings are more likely to be correctly interpreted across cultural divides? How many Western Europeans will correctly identify the prevailing mood of a musical passage from a Japanese opera? or a Persian classical song? And why is music then robbed of the status of being our "universal pastime and delight?" – an attribute saved by Longfellow for his own métier?

If we stay with the idea of metaphor – equating music with the way words are strung together to express some meaning - then we need to clarify to which form of verbal expression we are referring. For me, the greatest flaw in Lerdahl & Jackendoff's famous approach in *A Generative Theory of Tonal Music* (1983) was the fact that the linguistic model used was that of common prose. As a result, there was no room in their analyses for ambiguity of musical phrases. It is easy to argue that a poetic model would have made a better starting point (though it would probably have meant abandoning the majority of the book's contents). Some music has patterns of accents and even rhyme that fit the traditional molds quite well,[57] though the problems associated with expanding a poetic foot to the level of hypermeter were soon identified. Even more powerful than associating musical structures with traditional poetic form, however, is the analogy of free verse, where certain words and word combinations are chosen for their evocative qualities (often inextricably linked with their sounds) and arranged without regard for conventions of syntax. Other possibly appropriate models are likewise found (not surprisingly) within the realm of art: the stream-of-consciousness style of Virginia Woolf, for example, or

---

57. As Cooper & Meyer had already illustrated (1960).

the lifelike representation of conversations in a few films where interruptions and half-uttered phrases are common.

There are three more aspects of linguistic metaphors that seem potentially quite rich. One is semiotics, which – like many fields that emerge from the language / communication side of academia – is prone to much jargon. (And there is a fourth aspect, worthy of at least an evening's speculation: what is the musical equivalent of jargon?) However, those who understand both semiotics and music at a deep level (such as Jean-Jacques Nattiez - see for ex. Nattiez 2001) can offer useful models and perspectives for analysis.

Rhetoric is another area that has been occasionally revisited, and it seems clear that, as rhetorical technique was responsible for considerable amounts of Baroque compositional decisions, it would therefore be sensible to introduce the topic before moving into analytical mode of such works.

And a third, but scarcely-visited, potential link between musicology and linguistics is that of the archaeo-linguists, who study the evolution of language based on a combination of ancient written records with the traces of those languages as manifest in current dialects thought to be their descendants. As much of this research is based on aural-oral evidence, and combined with traces of cultural traditions and diasporas, it can provide some stimulating models for our own speculations on the music of our ancestors. For example, it seems that much more could be undertaken to promote an awareness, and further study, of the musical influence of Persian, Arabic, and North African music on the Iberian Renaissance music, and subsequently Western European as a whole – just as the study of "Celtic" music could be enhanced by comparative studies of folk tunes from vast regions of Europe from Prague to Portugal where one can discover strong traces of the Celtic tribes who were dominant for a millennium, and present for much longer.

In the modern world, a reflection on the use of footnotes, and now hyperlinks, is an interesting phenomenon that can make a written text much more efficient.[58] Tangents or additional clarifications can be reserved for a second reading, or, if one becomes 'side-tracked' by the footnote or link, one can return to the original place and if necessary re-read the text to that point. This is not so applicable in speech - unless in a dramatic situation one has a commentator (such as a Greek chorus), preferably in another tone of voice. However, attempting to establish a parallel in music leads me to imagine a fairly typical configuration in 20th-century works at least, where a main theme or texture can be interrupted or counterpointed with another idea, and the listener can clearly distinguish between them.

On the topic of metaphors in general, I am indebted to a keynote speech by Mark Johnson[59] for urging a reflection on the enormous potency of metaphor for expression. Once one begins to entertain the idea that music can be an appropriate means to explore metaphors of time, and even revealing the possible behaviours of time, then applying metaphors of language to music seems fertile, but not exhaustive.

On the topic of language in general, it is worth reiterating that language is often used as a weapon or an excuse between people who don't really want to communicate with those from other camps (see Ch. 2). Written language has long been used to discriminate the educated from the uneducated, and to imply that the

---

58. Though ironically, as I discovered, difficult in basic e-book formats.

59. Oslo, 1999.

uneducated are therefore stupid, whereas in fact they may be quite perceptive and articulate in oral communication (similar to the notation-illiterate musical performer, whose verbal explanation of a musical work may lag considerably behind her/his ability to demonstrate it sonically). Sometimes it seems that entire fields are dominated by those whose love of written language and new words or new definitions has led them to construct complicated frameworks where, when distilled to their essence, very little new revelations are made. Of course, new terminologies and concepts are essential, but when they cannot be easily explained to an intelligent outsider, then they may merit re-thinking.

25. Why would anyone want to study music by dead people? (or: How to approach contemporary music with enthusiasm)

It is relatively easy to demonstrate that diversity is one of the major features of 20th-century music, not only in overall sound, but in style, technique, instrumentation, performance venues, etc. Likewise, in music theory and analysis, there has been a proliferation of perspectives that can be seen as an echo of that diversity. Therefore, it should be possible to find contemporary music for everyone's taste. Nevertheless, one still encounters people who say that they "don't like" (or "don't understand") 'contemporary music'. Do they really mean everything musical produced in their lifetime? This becomes particularly depressing when these people happen to be professional musicians or music professors. Equally alarming is when one discovers that, for some musicians, 'contemporary music' includes composers like Debussy, Stravinsky, and Schoenberg... implying that they 'inherited' their dislike of contemporary music from their teachers' teachers' teachers.

It seems much more understandable that someone might not appreciate music from an earlier century or foreign culture - insofar as there are aspects of the musical language that may be difficult to grasp, and even be considered 'out of tune' or otherwise unacceptable in one's own tradition. In fact, this provides a parallel to the case of contemporary music. A person who has been weaned on modern renditions of Beethoven and Mozart, and told repeatedly that making funny vocal noises as a child is uncivilized, may well believe that the Western classical tonal language is the "right" one and that any music that does not follow its syntax is nonsense.

129

At a conference I attended, one presenter was trying to explain the difficulty of grasping the meaning of electroacoustic music because of the unfamiliarity of some of the sounds used. As part of his explanation, he mentioned that we learn language before we learn music. However, as my husband pointed out, we are subjected to some very odd loud noises while still in the womb, and as young children are as fully exposed to the noise of doors, food preparation, washing dishes, traffic, wind, etc. as we are to language. In addition, if we extend 'learning' music to 'listening to' music, as that is presumably a first stage, it would be surprising to find many infants within Western societies at least who have not been subject to music of some type before they begin to understand much language. And as the quality (compositional, performance, recording, playback) of the music is crucial to the development of a good ear, one can understand why some of us cringe at the banal and 'cheesy' music provided in some children's toys.

Part of the problem is that with contemporary music - and in fact with the last century of music in general - the less well crafted, less interesting, less coherent works have not yet been filtered out, so that someone trying to learn the languages of new music will have a noisy environment that precludes understanding.[60] In addition, the languages themselves are numerous – few children are exposed to more than, for example, three languages in intensive contact, whereas the languages of 20th-century music are more numerous than that. Imagine for example listening to works by Bacewicz, Varèse, Berg, Feldman, Stockhausen, Reich, Rzewski, Smalley, Oliveros; then add Cage, Alizadeh, Piazzolla, Abou-Khalil; then Mingus, Joplin, Jarrett, Stones, ELP, ... and a variety of art, folk

---

60. By this I refer to the metaphor of the communication theory 'signal-to-noise' ratio, where the number of poorly-constructed and unrewarding works far outweigh the better, more articulate ones.

and pop music from various cultures. Contemporary composers who were nurtured during the "sixties" are particularly eager to create their own 'distinct' sound, so this proliferation of styles begins compounding. We have composers who were influenced by Jimi Hendrix and John Cage, and hardly ever listened to Wagner - and others who were influenced by John Adams and Rachmaninoff, and hardly ever listened to Stockhausen.

In the early days, it was very difficult to have a musical work 'published' by an editor or record producer. Clearly, politics was often involved, but it did mean that many of the weaker compositions - and the occasional gem - was much harder to encounter. Nowadays, just about anyone can produce a CD and certainly put something on the web, so this first filter is no longer in place. This is wonderful in some ways, as it allows for many innovations to be accessible by a much wider audience. But it seems that such freedom would benefit from more accompanying recommendations by those of us who have been trained to appreciate the most varied of modern repertoire. Otherwise, people's information will be largely biased by commercial pressures that are even more arbitrary than the political pressures of the old record-producers' editorial boards. In the spirit of encouraging reflection on this issue, I have proposed that all responsible highly-trained musicians should be encouraged to cull their music collections (even digital ones) periodically, throw away the bad and boring pieces, and bequeath their favourites, in their wills, to libraries and resource centres, preferably, but even to favourite grandchildren, etc. This simple (if time-consuming) procedure would help (re-) establish standards of excellence, however biased. It would presumably also be useful to be more acknowledging about aesthetics as well (see Ch. 27); my own preferences, for example, are definitely coloured by particular levels of complexity, including for example polyrhythmic structures at micro- and macro-levels, as well as by a presence of non-tempered tunings and a certain degree of wit. Therefore, if there were catalogues that classified their works with these as perceptible parameters, it would help me find new works more quickly. Conversely, those for whom non-tempered systems is a source of irritation (typical of someone raised on 19th-century piano repertoire diet), then they would benefit from being spared all of those pieces that I love, until they are feeling particularly bold and ready to be re-trained (perhaps, for example, in music based on speech, which would be rooted in the familiar). Too much training, from children's music lessons through graduate courses in university, strongly discourages personal opinions - on the grounds, presumably, that the good students will learn to like everything pronounced good – so the acknowledgement of personal aesthetic taste is undervalued.

There are numerous CDs that try to educate the more traditional listener by placing a 20th-century piece on an album otherwise focussing on 19th- or 9th- century works. However, this often backfires, as the style of the more modern one can seem so dissonant that the listener will find her-/himself hesitant to play the whole thing, in order to avoid the jarring effect. (Of course, this can be remedied by different folders on one's computer.) This effect may be not merely an aesthetic dislike, but a dissonance between the style and even the function of the different tracks, so the listening mode may therefore be quite at variance.

In particular, it seems that any budding analyst in particular has three reasons for developing an interest in contemporary music: (1) it is part of our own world, and therefore can be better understood, as we are closer to understanding the environment in which it was made; (2) one is likely to be able to find and talk with at least some active participants in the field, who can often shed some light on our observations, and sometimes give valuable insights; and (3) the contemporary composers especially are in need of more discussion: feedback, observations, commentaries, and if possible critical analysis – most of all to help their potential audiences.

26. When and why did aesthetics become suspect?

AESTHETICS: rules and guidelines of style that are very rarely discussed but often shared within communities, and used by them to reject those whose tastes do not match their own.

I took a course in aesthetics in my first year of university - as my one non-music elective - and remember very little of it. However, more surprising than that is that I have rarely heard the word mentioned since. More recently, at a conference of Electroacoustic Music Studies[61] the keynote speaker Lars-Gunnar Bodin mentioned the word again with the rather justifiable complaint that it had not been approached during three days of talk about "meaning".

The problem is very much linked to the fact that aesthetics are personal, and not shared by all one's colleagues. Friends, on the other hand, often do share aesthetic tastes; or, to put it another way, those who do not share aesthetic tastes may find their friendship more strained. With good friends, even if the aesthetic taste is not shared, we do seem to be able to recognize it - how else would we be able to choose the perfect present for them on their birthdays? Again, our vocabulary and focus is partly to blame. If emotions are disregarded (see ch.18) then why do we care what our impressions are on hearing a piece of music?

It is interesting to reflect on to what extent aesthetics are cross-modal. If Mme. Y shares a preference for several musical compositions with Senhor X, is it likely that they will also share a preference for the same paintings? films? (My

61. EMS-2012, Stockholm.

experience is yes - non-shared areas are generally related to our differing childhood & adolescent experiences.)

It may be a bit difficult to accept, when we find something very beautiful or appealing or elegant, that not everyone else finds it so. It is also very difficult to explain why we do find it so - in fact, it is probably quite impossible. And yet it is that sense of aesthetics that drives us to create things in a certain way, and to appreciate things others have created. One psychologist, on contemplating our IMP project,[62] suggested that perhaps we could ascertain various different but definable "aesthetic profiles" in humans. Given the preponderance of the 'magical number seven' (Miller's Law), I suspect that we might indeed discover that there are 5-9 general categories.

Doubtless, experience and exposure has something to do with aesthetics, but it is not entirely responsible. Any visit to a museum or art gallery with a small group of people will evoke differing responses – even by people with extremely similar backgrounds. It seems to have become rather unfashionable for people to talk about the beauty of something because they will be attacked - or worse, shunned - by those who do not agree. There are of course those who don't want to find anything beautiful, but this seems more revealing of an emotional than an aesthetic sense. Most of us will find some things beautiful (or elegant, or whimsical), so presumably we should be able to listen to someone else describing what aspects they find beautiful without having to agree on the details, but rather to give us further ability to describe things that we find beautiful.

Another reason, of course, is that there has long been a group of people who insist that beauty has nothing to do with art. This seems a ridiculous extension from the quite acceptable opinion that not all art has to be

---

62. See Appendix D.

beautiful. Sometimes an artist may feel that a statement needs to be made that concerns reality and waking people up to what they might find unacceptable situations. As such, representing an ugly aspect of life may be felt to be necessary. However, to my mind, someone who feels that beauty is not a desirable part of life is rather perverted. I do realize that I may be fairly isolated in this opinion, as it seems that we are surrounded increasingly by a world that does not place a high enough value on beauty or other aesthetic values – though it seems more prevalent in North America where the exquisite beauty of much of the landscape has become increasingly substituted by human-made structures that consider aesthetics an unnecessary budget detail. Wandering around downtown Toronto and downtown Madrid, for example, one can be struck by the differences where the imagination and architectural detail of buildings seems so much richer in the latter (despite some contemporary Spanish architects deploring what they consider too much outmoded style). It is hard to believe that the predominance of less-than-interesting buildings in North American cities does not have a long-term, if subtle, negative effect on the development of aesthetic taste - to say nothing of the Canadian practice of charging high prices for gallery visits in contrast with the often free entries in Europe. We find this frequently in different cultures: some are far more willing to pretend that aesthetics are a luxury rather than an essential part of daily existence.

For me, aesthetics has to do with colour, texture, proportion, and form as much as 'content'; in musical terms, this involves the actual timbres (of instruments or electronically-produced sounds), the temporal proportions, the avoidance of 'jarring' amplitude bursts, etc. Is this widespread?

Aesthetics are often shared by sub-cultures - people with similar upbringings, ages, cultural references, etc.

136

Therefore, they seem to create means by which exclusive groups are formed - thus closely linked to a means by which someone may be ostracized as not sharing the same tastes. As a result, perhaps there is considerable insincerity involved in the subject, whereby people pretend that they like some things so that they will be accepted into a particular group.

Is there a hierarchy of aesthetic tastes? Perhaps, but that does not mean that there is only one set of aesthetics that is the highest: more likely, in any aesthetic grouping, there are more refined and less refined tastes. Therefore, people should be encouraged - even as young children - to express their opinion on artistic things, and not be ridiculed for them. I was surprised, during the one year when I taught piano to young children, that my students were delighted that I asked them to choose which pieces they wanted to play (from a fairly restricted list in the conservatory book); they had not realized that they might be allowed to voice their opinions.

Similarly, it took me many years - well past graduate studies - before I was honest enough to admit, even to myself, that I have a distinct preference for music written in modes other than major; as major is considered the 'basic' one in Western music, this meant that I had to admit that about 80% of the pieces I was presented with as a student were less interesting to me. And it seemed, given the lack of acceptance of having aesthetic preferences, that this was too simplistic and superficial an attribute of the music to be allowed to affect my opinion. However, by not recognizing this, I had to go to great lengths to try and find other more 'valid' reasons for my lack of interest. Similarly, I have a great fondness for harpsichord timbres - presumably connected to an appreciation for much of the music written for harpsichord - which means that I will be far more tolerant of a harpsichord piece even if its formal structure in the end seems lacking in interest. However, I am also well aware that the same timbre is immediately irritating to many people, who may well enjoy the same works played on piano. Who is right? Both - or, in fact, the question is wrong. It is not a question of right or wrong but of aesthetic preference. It seems, in conclusion, that more appreciation of the divergence of aesthetic taste, and less effort to despise those whose taste differs from our own, or from the 'mainstream', would greatly benefit our conversations about other aspects of musical or artistic output.

27. Why is pedagogy not an integral part of learning? (or: The art of exploring)

It is a great mystery why the university professor is never taught to teach. A prevalent view among academics I have met is that the "music ed[ucation] people" oversimplify, or avoid main issues and topics as irrelevant, preferring to ignore the joys of the complex and the intricate. There does seem to be a tendency in this direction, symbolized for me in various "educational" preferences like the overabundance of solid primary colours, keyboards, and rather insipid tonal (major) tunes. However, surely if more scholars in other areas spared some thought for pedagogy, we might have more input into the early training of future scholars. And the writings of those who have thought long and deep about teaching music, even though often focussed on the elementary and high school levels[63] should presumably be standard reading for university music professors - especially now that 'common practice' would more aptly refer to listening to non-classical music through earphones or trying to create interesting sonic material on one's computer or digisynth. In fact, I would argue that any PhD programme in music, which is now the accepted minimum requirement for university teaching, should include at least one course on pedagogical issues, strategies, trends, and creative proposals for the future.

Much of my own teaching style evolved from my determination not to imitate some of my own teachers: my piano teacher, who scolded me for laughing at what I recognized years later to be a harmonic joke in Debussy's *Arabesque I*; my first-year music history teacher, apologizing

---

63. Such as Reimer, Alperson, Allsup, Elliott, Silverman, and the various journals of music education and philosophy of music education in different countries.

to the class that we had to listen to some odd music and then playing Palestrina - and who chose a textbook as appalling as the pre-Palisca Grout (which sneered at Mendelssohn for lacking harmonic complexity and dismissed Messiaen in one paragraph); my first composition teacher, who sat down at the piano and tried to sight-read my new piece for unpitched percussion, but with considerable mistakes in the rhythms - and then gave me a poor mark; or the interim Ph.D. advisor (who did not himself have a doctorate) who thought that I should accept bureaucratic hassles as a valid substitute for intellectual challenges. In addition, I am skeptical of curricula or methodologies designed for the "average person", or, more commonly, the designer's personal acquaintances, whether they be music theory professors or software designers. Therefore, the essential need to ensure a diversity of evaluation methods (recommended by experts in pedagogy) is still widely ignored. Hopefully, memorizing readily-accessible facts over testing comprehension is not as common as it used to be.

I can only assume that professors are too fearful of their own fates if more reflection were encouraged on teaching methodology. And tenure has become so embedded that a really poor professor is often withdrawn from the classroom to become department chair . . . which reminds me that the lack of administrative training for academics is almost as crippling for most universities as the lack of pedagogical training.

My proposals:

Since "pedagogy" seems to suggest pre-university teaching, maybe we can focus instead on the "*arts of exploration*". I was quite startled, years ago, to come across a comment that the word "explore" had etymological links to the idea of "crying out" about one's findings, suggesting that exploration is not complete without sharing what one has discovered. Therefore, a focus on *the arts of exploration* would have to include a range of activities such as discovering, evaluating, presenting, and explaining.[64] These would capture much of the essence of what we need to learn as effective teachers; it would also presuppose some reflection on the diversity of personality types and learning strategies that might make up one's audience. Those who are going to teach children or teenagers can then add to this by studying relevant issues from developmental psychology.

Improving one's *discovery* skills would presumably include the type of research methodologies (usually addressed, rather belatedly, in the first year of graduate studies), but could also address strategies for determining how to choose one's research or knowledge focus, and should involve some consideration of the growing issues of information overload and strategies of retrieval, at least at the conceptual level. It could also include, for musicologists, some consideration of how to use imagination to supplement the incomplete information provided by a score, recording, or book.

This is intimately connected with some aspects of the art of *evaluating,* which should include critical and analytical techniques useful for reading scholarly texts, listening to lectures, and analyzing scores and performances -- in addition to the general guidelines for assessing a student's progress. As *presenting* can embrace music performance and visual content as well as verbal and written words, and should acknowledge the medium (concert, classroom, web, journal, etc.), its study would help draw attention to the shared and individual characteristics of each format.

---

64. Within pedagogical research, there are several variations of organizing learning. The usefulness, I believe, is in creating such divisions - see Ch. 32.

Becoming adept at the art of *explaining* (which I think of as inevitably involving language) would be invaluable for any interdisciplinary (or inter-sub-disciplinary) discourse as well as for the more obvious contexts of curriculum delivery and published research.

It seems that any resistance to including pedagogical concerns into a music curriculum would have difficulty in arguing against courses -- or at least course content -- dealing with exploration, so perhaps this could be a first step towards more effective transfer of knowledge.

28. The benefits and perils of collaboration

Collaboration is a very common ingredient of many artforms, but is found much more rarely in traditional research. Collaboration can take many forms: it is quite rare for two composers to join together on creating a piece - but several composers may join forces to present their works together, just as some artists might have a group show. More typically, a composer might collaborate with a film-maker, or a choreographer, or a librettist, in order to produce an artistic work with a music component. The most common form of collaboration is that between composers and performers, and among the various performers (including the conductor) themselves. The performer's role in conveying the 'message' of the music is often under-valued (by composers and musicologists), but when one acknowledges their fundamental part in acoustic music, one can see that their role is akin to a real collaboration even if the composer belongs to a different time-period. In other words, a convincing performance demands a certain sympathy with the creator's intentions for the objective of presenting the work.

In research, one might argue that collaboration exists in the participation in societies and conferences where members share their findings in an effort to promote general understanding of the topics. However, although this can work effectively in very small groups of 20-30 researchers focussing on a single theme (such as a single composer or methodology), where there is a sincere desire to listen, share, and learn through a building of understanding, such traits are less typical of large groups where personalities, politics, and competitiveness often drive wedges into the collaborative tendencies that characterize many honest researchers.

143

Multi-modal collaborations such as film, dance, art installations, gaming, etc. - where collaboration is involved on the level of creation / production - depends on some degree of inter-disciplinary dialogue, so the issues that are encountered correspond to those discussed in this book. Therefore, collaboration among a small group of analysts and critics from different fields could be appropriate for appraising such a multi-modal artwork, as each component artform has its own frameworks for discussion.[65] Some fascinating insights can be provided into apparently 'uni-modal' instrumental works by a parallel way, when for example a Baroque dance suite is studied both in terms of its music and its original dance-form, drawing on the expertise of analysts in music and dance.

Co-authored articles are extremely common in the sciences and many bridge areas like psychology. It seems logical to assume that more encouragement for musicians to participate in such collaborations would be worthwhile. More mixing of performers, composers, and people from neighbouring disciplines at the start of an investigation, instead of at the conclusion, might help the participants learn the nuances of each other's language and concerns.

My imagined profile of Conversational Musicologists is one that would be necessarily collaborative to some extent - as the Conversational Musicologist would have to be in close touch with at least one researcher from each sub-discipline with which they are developing expertise.

---

65. This kind of exploration is most frequently found in art circles (often, however, with less musical expertise) and within the emerging field of Performance Studies.

SECTION V:

OTHER TOPICS FOR REFLECTION

29. Data mining, music classification & retrieval

There are some basic questions about music classification and retrieval that affect all of us, yet this remains an area where we have little discussion outside the specialists of ISMIR [International Society for Music Information and Retrieval]. Many of those specialists are particularly interested in computer-based systems, often in an artificial intelligence capacity (originally on the interesting though questionable ground that what we can't teach a computer to do, we don't thoroughly understand). One of the main ways in which we interact with these systems (or lack thereof) is on the internet, while searching for some music. Music classification systems are starting to proliferate on the web, as people want to go to a site and find something appropriate to download. In YouTube, for example, calling up a particular video will also call up numerous other "suggestions". These are often very clearly related – the next few episodes in the same series of a TV programme, for example, or other movies / videos featuring the same principal actress / performer. Sometimes the links seem more tenuous. Very often, they are not aesthetically related - although companies are trying to figure this out.

Genre seems like the obvious way to classify music – pop, rock, jazz, classical.... but also of little use to those of us in contemporary music, because when do we call it classical and when is it free jazz? Even in pop music, it is of very limited use, because there are millions of selections, so it is only really useful to separate out the classical and jazz unless one is using names – in which case, a simple search may suffice. One finds out that many of the boundaries are blurry (e.g. when does pop-rock become pop?) and many of the definitions are regional. What someone in Delhi

146

might consider 'pop' will probably be considered 'world' by someone in Arkansas. Also, huge computer systems necessarily aim towards a common denominator – and those of us with a strong interest in 'classical' music are not a large percentage of the internet population. Therefore, even if a system is devised that pleases 80% of the people 80% of the time, it will probably not help me – nor my potential fans.

A simple example of the problem is how one stores one's CDs in the house. Are they organized chronologically? by country? by genre? by composer? by performer? by favourites? a combination? Perhaps you have only mp3s on the computer now – have you taken the time to tag them all with appropriate tags? Or have you accepted those assigned to them by someone you don't know?

I have spoken elsewhere (2004) about the foolishness of marketing computer music as 'computer music' because it says nothing about the genre or the aesthetic. I proposed that we might want to have labels describing the salient features – but what are these? Presumably, they are a bit different for different people, and depend also on the context. Are you looking for a piece to play while washing the dishes, or to provide a nice atmosphere for your friends coming for dinner, to give you a model for a film score you are working on, or simply an old-fashioned desire for both intellectual and sensory enjoyment?

One demonstration of information retrieval problems emerges when working with the sound effects libraries that are found in film schools and such places. Often, there will be thousands of these, categorized by apparently very sensible means: trains – steam, electric, whistles; subways; cars – racing, city traffic, honk; birds – forest, field, flock; etc. But how does one find what one wants? Several of my students reported that in the end, it was simply easier to take the sound recorder and find their own sounds. That makes sense – but then one has the problem in one's own computer when beginning to identify them as they become manipulated and saved:

- car1.wav
- car2.wav
- car2a.wav
- car2a-slowed40pc.wav,
- car2a-slowed40pc-granulation.wav ....

etc.

It seems a growing problem, without adequate means of solving it yet. The main point is probably to recognize that there will not be a single perfect system, but rather that there will be several, depending on context, culture, genre, etc. Probably there is not an infinite number either, so it may be possible to find some basic system models (maybe 5?) and then some basic variants (maybe 9?) I propose that it can be useful to chat about sorting in general – especially when one has full latitude to employ one's own strategies - such as jigsaw puzzles. Do other jigsaw puzzle enthusiasts sort pieces the same way as I do? Are those with a more sophisticated vocabulary for shades of colour at an advantage? How many effective systems are there?

30. Music & architecture

Sounds suggest space, and spaces shape sound. A few years ago I became involved with researchers in Montreal and Madrid[66] working on this theme, and it is one of those areas where one can't imagine, afterwards, what life was like beforehand.

Musicians and architects seem to share various characteristics: working with abstract forms, striving for aesthetic solutions, often showing an affinity for mathematics, etc. But in some ways they are quite different in their work: architecture is very much a practical, visible three-dimensional form, bound by gravity and the properties of various physical materials and forces, and the potential effect of the environment and all the people and contents and activities. In addition, it needs to be functional, in a more mundane way than music. (Xenakis mentions this as an attraction for his switching of professions.) Musicians, on the other hand, seem bound by nothing except the constraints of sound – which are really only theoretical, in that anything that makes a sound is useable as a sound source (whether an oscillator or two stones) – coupled with our perceptual limits (in terms of loudness, frequency range, and rhythmic discernibility). We don't have to understand physics, and the only physical constraints of humans we need to think about are the limitations of the performer and, preferably, some perceptual/ phenomenological issues. Interestingly, since instrument design evolved to allow humans to play sonic configurations that would be perceptible, the composer who stays within traditional performance practice does not need to calculate perceptual limins to the same degree. Of course we may wish to think

---

66. Diego Agudelo-Gallo, in Montreal, and José Luis Carles and Cristina Palmese, at the Universidad Autónoma de Madrid and Universidad Europea de Madrid, respectively.

about the desires of the audiences, but that is a different question.

However, the combination of music with architecture is quite fascinating. Music in fact suggests architecture in that every musical work has two aspects of space: the space of the performance (which may be created or altered synthetically); and the space suggested by the sounds themselves – open, closed, dark, light, serpentine, immense, etc.

Architecture, in its way, naturally affects the sounds that are in and around it. These are usually thought of in terms of acoustics, and acoustics to most of us suggests the dimensions of a hall where we might want to talk, or perform. But an entire building – whether the Alhambra or a factory on the outskirts of town – has its own acoustic properties that may encourage or discourage certain types of behaviour. From encouraging songbirds through space and landscape design to discouraging conversation by overly-resonant close surfaces, each building can impose some shape on the sounds around it. The materials of building can be part of a personal aesthetic preference in terms of how it affects sounds as much as its visual appeal. Many of us have a distinct preference for concert venues (and living spaces) full of wood panelling and irregularity of surface rather than, for example, rectangular or cubic rooms with an abundance of concrete and plastic. On the other hand, a tiled courtyard with a pond could provide a suitable setting for certain instruments and repertoire. Would this not make for a suitable topic within a music curriculum?

31. Acoustic ecology (or: When will we have quiet shoe stores?)

It would be irresponsible to conclude a book such as this without mentioning some of the issues commonly embraced by the term "acoustic ecology", or sometimes 'soundscape". As pointed out by Rudi (2013), several of those involved with acoustic ecology are politically driven and thus tend to simplify their arguments to win their points. He mentioned aspects like their invasion of silent and pristine wilderness with noisy vehicles, ugly equipment, and debris of human camps, in the name of championing the silence and peacefulness of the scene. What is true about this complaint is that some of these people have a kind of self-righteousness that can lose them 'followers'. A similar complaint is hurled against R. Murray Schafer, who coined the exceedingly useful term 'soundscape' and did much to launch a movement of more awareness of the sounds in the environment, along with his colleagues in the World Soundscape Project. Although many people, including myself, found his book *The Tuning of the World* very stimulating and thought-provoking, it has been criticized, sometimes severely, for some of its content and delivery. One of the problems is simply that he was writing in a style that was familiar to him in order to explain some points, which were as often expressed in a more poetic sense than rigorously, and without much precedence for the discourse. We were therefore fortunate to have Truax's book *Acoustic Communication* which took some of the central points and formulated them in a different language style and with arguments based on a different set of disciplinary research which could then reach different people. The same could be said of another Soundscape explorer, Hildegard Westerkamp, whose "soundwalks" reached yet a different public through a more direct sensitizing through audio.

However, the point remains that most of the Western public tries to ignore the very non-musical sounds of our environment. Why? Perhaps because we don't know how to fight those who are making it ugly: car manufacturers who insist on fossil fuels because that's how they make their money, etc. But some of it also is simply a very ancient use of sound as power – if you want to stress your importance around the tribe, make lots of noise when you enter. Of course, the vast difference is that in the ancient tribal times, there were only two or three contenders for such a position, and only for a short period of time before one was chosen or conquered; therefore, the noise was quite restricted to special occasions on the chief's entry into prime position. Now in our over-populated world, we have every middle-class ladder-climber jockeying for position, and many of them using sound as part of their arsenal. It is probably safe to conclude that all drivers of boomer cars are bullies – and frankly, parallel to many store and hotel managers who put on loud pop music in semi-public places. For store managers, however, it is more complex: many really seem to believe that music will help attract customers. In the case of a club, it is true that loud music of a certain genre will clearly identify the aesthetics of the place, and keep certain types of people (like me) out, which is the goal. But when a similar music, at a similar volume, is played in a shop that sells hardware or stationery supplies, it makes no sense. Have the manufacturers of all those sinks and floor tiles agreed that they want to sell their wares only to people of a certain aesthetic profile – usually young and without the funds to spend on such mundane items? More likely, it is simply an example of 10th-hand information deriving from popular accounts of psychological tests – many of which were not properly vetted in the first place – coupled with the very prevalent but faulty notion that if so many others are doing it, it must be OK.[67]

So, what do we do? One excellent example was PipeDown – an English organization that simply went out and conducted surveys and managed, for example, to convince Heathrow Airport to stop playing Muzak-type sounds. They also published a directory of British pubs that did not play music.[68] Personally, I think that every town should have this kind of directory – and would welcome "silent Tuesdays" or some such scheme whereby the majority of shops in a town would turn their 'ambient music' off for a particular day or half-day (perhaps rotating) and see what happens to their sales. Otherwise, we have more and more people walking around with headphones (or sometimes earplugs, but that I think is more rare) so that they can block out unwanted sounds with the sounds of their choice.

The effect of noise in our environment is clearly linked with a high level of anxiety. A simple test of this is to go with a very good friend and spend a week in a quiet place. There are not so many left on this planet – even in very isolated places one is often disturbed with airplanes – but places like the Badlands of Alberta or the open fields of Soria in Spain still preserve areas of silence and allow small sounds (such as the popping open of seed pods, or the beating wings of small birds) to be appreciated. Another thing mentioned by Rudi was that silence is not an integral part of all natural landscapes – consider for example the rain forest with a cacophony of sounds – and that therefore

---

67. A more frightening suspicion is that the sounds played over the speakers are mere carriers or shields for more perverse sonic signals designed to affect behaviour in certain ways.

68. The Wetherspoon chain of pubs made the intelligent policy to ban 'ambient music' from the vast majority of their venues, which doubtless contributes to their popularity by allowing conversations to flourish.

we should not assume that it is the preferred 'zero' state. Yet I cannot believe that a good periodic dose of silence is not beneficial for most people of the world – although many urban dwellers are likely to spend the first couple of days in a quiet environment feeling very anxious, as they are not used to it. As a composer, silence provides me a 'blank slate' which is important or even vital at a certain early stage of composing. For days I will refuse to listen to any music at all, and then, if living in a cramped space, need to take batteries out of clocks and turn the refrigerator off for a few hours so that I do not have to fight against their persistent interruptions. Should I really have to travel over a thousand miles every time I want to have silence outside my room as well?

The first step may be to talk about this, and the second to protest. That the talk should happen within music programmes as well as elsewhere seems clear. If people spend their lives learning how to 'tune out', then presumably they will not be the best audiences. We should be able to have some expert teachers within the music training industry who can provide students with very solid information and thereby arm them for proper battles when necessary. National Express buses in the UK and even many of the buses in Spain are now much stricter about music than they were 20 years ago (in the sense that their clientele should not be subject to random musical choices by others). Now we need specific shopping malls – even towns – where quiet environments become a tourism-enhancing commodity. Meanwhile, every time one is in a restaurant, hotel, or shop where the music seems objectionable, why not complain? Alternatively, one could follow the wry advice of a cynical staff member at my university and buy shares in the hearing aid companies....

32. Music of the spheres (for the spaceships; for the aliens; by the aliens...)

The music of the spheres is often presented as a rather charming example of how naïve our ancestors were. Everything on earth reflecting the order of the universe – how quaint! It was therefore startling for me to learn about Kepler and his discovery of the asteroid belt: he was apparently looking for a planet that should have been in that orbit, according to his calculations based on the harmonic series. (One assumes that his task was made a bit easier by the imprecision of his measurements: in a rough sense, the approximations to simple ratios between orbits are more apparent than when working with very precise calculations of distance.)

A few more scraps of evidence that support the idea of the music of the spheres, at least as a concept for grasping the beauty and complexity of life's structures, are being entertained in the science world now under the terms of fractals and string theory. Fractals, in showing the degree to which a similar structure can be observed at different 'zoom' levels of the same natural thing (mountains, trees, coastline), seem to support the idea of *musica mundana* and *musica universalis* – especially if one understands that not all mountains nor all trees have the same structure, although they may share some aspects per group. String theory is even more entrancing because it embeds the idea of vibration into the structuring of universal time. When taken along with J.T. Fraser's ideas about the evolution of time, this produces a nice concept: perhaps each nth vibration triggers an evolutionary wave.

Another curious proposal is that sound must be the origin of all of the complexities of life's designs, because one can see the shapes of organic beings materialize through

155

beaming different sonic configurations (i.e. chords) onto a plate with sand, for example, and watching them take the shapes of familiar organisms (e.g. a trilobyte). This area (called cymatics) is a fascinating one to explore, although a problem with the argument is that it is somewhat *non sequitur* – even if a familiar shape can be caused by sound, is this clear evidence of how the world was devised? Maybe it was just the gods playing with sound who then found their source of design? But this is hardly an improvement on explaining.

Electroacoustic music, often filled with sounds for which we can imagine no earth-bound sound source, is often linked by novice listeners with science-fiction film tracks. In this way, the alien or extra-terrestrial gives us a framework for both grasping and communicating novel ideas – even more than trying to imagine a future world on earth, where we are increasingly bound by selective histories of the past millennia coupled with the rather dire dystopian versions proposed by Hollywood. Therefore, trying to imagine music by, and for, aliens could be a very valuable exercise in creativity for composers – and an exercise in mental gymnastics for the musicologist who has a hard time with the playful side of things.

33. The joys and dangers of charts and categories

> *There are two types of people in the world: those who divide the world into two types of people, and those who don't.* - Robert Benchley

The pastime of imagining the various ingredients of music and their interactions in meaningful ways can be a fascinating one. One attraction is the visual aspect of the charts and diagrams that are used to illustrate a classification system. A deeper appeal comes from reflecting on how closely an existing or proposed chart reveals the most efficient and accurate form of presentation. Charts and categories are, to some personalities, a natural product of trying to understand something and, if well-worked-out, can be exceedingly helpful in communicating something. They naturally appear as useful to research for those who enjoy both design and organization; in my own research they have been frequently-used tools.

However, there are good reasons to be skeptical of all charts. The benefits lie mainly in the exercise of drawing up new ones periodically throughout any given research project, if one is so inclined, because the attempts to categorize and see connections coax the inquisitive mind into so much reflection that the process far outweighs the finished design in importance. But, some diagrams group things together in predetermined numbers because their designers like the resulting symmetry. And if one is particularly fond of order and design, one is susceptible to proposing classifications that appear neat, rather than those which are the most accurate representation of the contents. In general, even if these superficial influences are suppressed, the specific choice of categories and organizational structures can reveal a specific mental construct. Often it is just this array of assumptions that goes un-noticed by both the transmitter and the viewer. Such constructs may be cultural, though sometimes it seems narrower than that: an accumulated tradition of musicologists or music psychologists, for example, developed in near isolation of their peers' reaction to music.

Just as making a chart can be stimulating in itself, examining someone else's for its strengths and weaknesses can be a satisfying mental exercise, as it leads to questions for cognitive scientists about how we think - about music and other things. It would therefore be nice to see more counter-proposals of the most interesting charts presented, partly on the grounds that re-designing a chart will involve a similar amount of thinking to that of creating the original.

One of the dangers is that a chart *can* be read very quickly, but *should* be read very slowly and thoughtfully. Likewise, a clear diagram appears to have distilled considerable amount of information into clear structures, and therefore appears less open to doubt and criticism than, for example, a rambling sentence which explains its author's reasoning and thereby allows us to trace the argument. But this is a danger, because charts are usually designed by individuals who are as prone to bias and error as the rest of us, and there may be a major flaw in the design; a missing set of parameters, or a lack of acknowledgement of changing conditions, for example. (With the increasing ease of animation tools, we will hopefully start to see charts that incorporate a temporal dimension - perhaps in the sense of an oscillation between two states, or a shifting of component relationships - which might be a more appropriate way of portraying most realities.) Probably the two most dangerous pitfalls of such diagrams are (i) omitting a key element (e.g. a category or a possibility) while purporting to be inclusive, and (ii) treating unequal elements as equal, e.g. in terms of their respective hierarchical levels.

On the other hand, if we encouraged students (and ourselves) to make charts of anything relevant, we might encourage a pleasant pastime, prettier summaries, better skills for evaluating existing diagrams, and the occasional insight.

34. The challenge of being a true amateur in a world being devoured by greed

The word 'amateur' in English seems generally disconnected from its original meaning of one who loves the subject. This disconnect is a pity. The prevalent view, in North America at least, seems to be: "If you're not doing it for money, you're not taking it seriously." (A related issue is believing that a concert will be valued by the community according to its ticket price.)

In my case, as with many of my contemporaries, there were several reasons to dismiss musical composition as a potential income source:

- self-marketing may be frowned on by one's community as being ill-mannered;

- many composers have been appreciated only years after death, so it is not really important to do more than leave one's scores in an accessible place for posthumous discovery;

- if one starts composing for financial gain, one sets oneself up for catering to public whim, which would taint the purer motivation of artistic expression;

- in some countries, such as Canada, organizations like the Canada Council helped make the public feel that artists do not need private support, whereas in fact the 'peer review' system became such a political & aesthetic clique that independent artists rarely, if ever, became recipients; etc.

Likewise, the disparaging category of "Sunday painters" could be re-thought as a more creative occupation than the more common "Sunday web surfer"; at least a "Sunday painter" who has only time one day a week to pursue his or her delight in artistic expression manages to prioritize that activity, whereas the "professional artist" is, in my experience, more likely to regard the production of artworks for his or her "public" (which may be a grant-subsidized network or a lucrative gallery) as approximating a more tedious "work" occupation.

The joy of being an amateur, of course, is that one does just what one wants. It tends to imply, also, that one has not had "professional" training: but what about those of us who have a Master's in composition and then never sought commissions or grants?

35. Finding the time for it all...

A major factor that many people try to downplay is lack of time. One simple if drastic remedy is to work in part-time or temporary situations so that one has the time to research properly, with 'quality time'. However, ironically, academia is loath to take seriously those who are not holding a full-time tenured position. And unless one is very fortunate, the financial challenge of such a solution can easily negate the benefits.

We have a limited number of hours in our lives – and an increasing number of things to occupy our time, or so it seems. There is also a crucial and related element of pacing – if one spends too many minutes or hours on a particular task, the tedium can cause one to lose the sense of purpose or concentration.

Often, the main culprit seems to be computer-related:

- **COMPLICATED COMPUTER SOFTWARE:** gone are the days of software designers striving to create 'elegant' programmes that would be set out with intuitive and customizable interfaces. Composition students come up with an interesting idea, and spend three hours fighting with the notation software, eventually giving in to its pressures to write 'square' melodies and accompaniments rather than playing with pen strokes to suggest note bends and multiple meters.

- **KEEPING UP WITH NEW HARDWARE & SOFTWARE:** many hours are spent researching the best deals on computers, sorting out warranty issues, learning software, updating software.... These are all things that never subtracted any time from undergraduate days or research weekends of us older folk.

- **INTERNET SEARCHES:** increasingly, as websites

multiply, and marketing becomes more aggressive, it is difficult to find relevant information on the web (although Wikipedia remains generally a wonderful exception). In a simple search engine, the number of pages of results that one needs to scan before encountering a relevant entry has increased, and even simple ones like looking for the name of a musicologist can lead to football stars, while acronyms of one's favourite conferences are seen to be identical to a myriad of unrelated toys and corporations. Those of us who remember libraries with shelves holding subject-related books remain nostalgic.

- **E-MAILS/SOCIAL NETWORKS:** one great advantage of conferences over e-mail discussions is that people are given equal amounts of time to talk, in the most articulate way possible, about the essence of their thoughts about what is important to them in their research at the current time. E-mail discussions, on the other hand, can have a very low signal-to-noise ratio (unless compared to the newer social networks), full of what we used to call "half-baked ideas". The worst part is that even if most of the participants are striving to keep the conversation on a high level, one or two members can easily dominate with garbage: comments aimed to divert attention to some insignificant or irrelevant issue, etc. In a physical conference, people can exchange glances, walk away and re-group somewhere else – which could happen on an e-mail discussion group too, except that walking away from one's computer is not so visible, nor are other visual cues, and re-grouping is not so simple (though it might be interesting to explore how to achieve this in the virtual world).

Even though one could cite the enormous variety of music available on the web as ample compensation for all of this, we had almost the same variety available to us in the late 1970's – not nearly as many pieces per genre, but nonetheless a manageable sampling – from well-stocked music libraries. The web as music archive is much more of an advantage to a professor who can now find and play pieces in class without having to arrive with a sore arm from dragging a pile of LPs from the library across campus – but this is a fairly minor consideration, surely? Other internet-related factors are our ability to connect instantly to the rest of the world (or so we are led to believe) that tends to create a sense of remaining un-informed if one is not connected. This is a more extreme version of what is happening in the academic world: the proliferation of books, articles, conferences, webpages, resource centres, and even university programmes makes one hesitate to do anything without reviewing it all. But of course, this is impossible, because once one has succeeded, the first resources one learned about will have become obsolete.

My long hesitation in publishing includes a reluctance to add to this flood, but if anyone finds the concepts in this book attractive or more accessible than their counterparts elsewhere, perhaps we can refine the topics I have presented into a slightly more comprehensive list (while keeping something of the same scale), refine also the different types of approaches, and begin exchanging thoughts in more effective ways, even when the members of the discussion are from different disciplines, areas, or perspectives. And some of us who are not more gainfully employed can declare ourselves Conversational Musicologists, and demonstrate the potential of such a role.

APPENDIX

A:

VARIOUS
SUB-DIVISIONS
OF
MUSICOLOGY

Sub-divisions of musicology

The following is a very crude guide to the various areas of musicology, though of course any practitioner of any of the sub-fields will be happy to offset my composer's bias with their own specialist's bias. The more one becomes immersed in any one sub-field, the more one is aware of all the little sub-sub-fields as well, along with the fluctuations of attention and growth (and wrong turns and dead-ends) that have occupied their members.

A musicologist may or may not be concerned about her/his methodology and designation. On the other hand, I imagine that a well-trained musicologist should be aware of all the different approaches to some extent, and have some idea how to choose the best approach in order to address the most interesting aspects of the music being studied. However, at the current pace, the way to achieve such familiarity is not obvious. This is the motivation for the proposed *Tool Kit* (see *Appendix B*). It would include a more detailed chart of the various sub-fields, with more keywords and (less subjective) descriptions, along with the titles of the various journals, organizations, and range of music that belong to each area. Part of the idea is to be able to view the whole field in various re-arrangements, until eventually the budding researcher would be able to enter any of the sub-fields without hesitation.

HISTORICAL MUSICOLOGY — focusses on examining the music, the composer, and sometimes the audience, the venue, etc. in terms of the socio-cultural history. As such, this branch shares many aspects (though fewer conferences and journals) with those in ethnomusicology, anthropology, art history, world or regional history, etc. The dangers with the historical approach are several: outside of the history of one's own culture and era, one is prone to misunderstanding of the context, due to differences of perception, language, society, etc. Also, the way in which history is usually approached incorporates a type of linearity that may be suspect: assumptions are often made to try to link events, trends, etc. with previous or concurrent events and trends, whereas they might be unrelated. This becomes quite a serious problem in the study of the 20th century, when so many currents coexist that a particular composer may be ignorant of some trends that are in his/her regional/temporal proximity, and be inspired by others from afar. (A fascinating analogy presented by Broyles [2000] is that of chaos theory as a model of 20th-century developments in music history.) A related and significant but more obscure problem is that composers or works that don't fit neatly into the accepted patterns of an historical progression are frequently dropped by historians, even if not by the contemporary audiences.

EMPIRICAL MUSICOLOGY – a relatively recent term for the branch of musicology based on observation, experience, or experiments.[69] This sub-field groups efforts in musicology that are influenced by procedures and perspectives more common to science, but introduced into the music field by people working in psychology, computation, statistics & data analysis, etc. It seems an attractive approach: as stated in the abstract to the first chapter of the book *Empirical Musicology*, they are trying to correct the problem of "musicologists [who] frequently work with very small amounts of data even where large data sets are available, resulting in findings that are less firmly grounded than they might be." There are deliberate links forged with sociology and music psychology among others. As the term is still new, the book cited above is mainly designed to define and

---

69. The *Empirical Musicology Review* was founded by David Huron and David Butler in 2004; and the Clarke/Cook book published the same year.

explain the field and its repercussions.

SYSTEMATIC MUSICOLOGY – also interdisciplinary, more on the humanities side, with aesthetics, semiotics, and musical criticism figuring within it. A good overview of the field is given by Parncutt (2007) and a comprehensive explanation in Schneider (2008).

COGNITIVE MUSICOLOGY – although it suggests simply musicology concerned with perception and cognition issues, it is often taken in quite a narrow view relating to knowledge representation and the use of computer modelling, thus overlapping significantly with the field of artificial intelligence (AI). However, the broader issues of music cognition are clearly embodied within such research.

MUSIC PSYCHOLOGY – although this appears to be a branch of psychology rather than musicology, much of the research that deals with perception and cognition issues, especially as relating to performance and audience reception, seems to emerge in this field. I explain in Ch. 23 why this area is also extremely relevant for composers. There is an overlap with an area called psycho-acoustics, dealing more specifically with perception of sounds in a narrower way and usually approached more from a physics standpoint; however, the field of music psychology also contains much research whose applications are farther from theory & analysis such as developmental psychology, pedagogy, etc.

COMPARATIVE MUSICOLOGY – although this term sounds like just the thing for examining the various approaches to music (as in 'comparing musicologies') it is generally used in the sense of being the precursor of ethnomusicology (that is, comparing music from different cultures), although Cook probes the term a bit further, and Schneider (2008) clarifies.

ETHNOMUSICOLOGY – the study of the music of

different ethnicities, or cultures. It therefore has huge overlaps with (and could be considered a subset of) anthropology, cultural studies, cultural geography, etc. One of the most striking pitfalls of ethnomusicology is its historical tendency to be a study of "other people's music" with a rather colonial stance. This shortcoming was spotted in the mid-20th century, along with a growing awareness of colonial bias, and spawned a lovely exercise wherein two ethnomusicologists turned the tables on their peers and applied ethnomusicological methods to a concert of Western classical music. Ethnomusicology was severely limited in the early days by being confined by inappropriate tools, developed initially to study Western European art music. Not only was the traditional notation system inadequate or clumsy for notating music outside the 12-tone equal temperament and common metric structures, but also the music might have different contexts, functions, and concepts: for example, rather than existing in a single "ideal" version, the music might be conceived of as a fuzzier notion linked more intricately to performance. Another great problem was that of recording technology: in an attempt to circumvent the notational problem, it was typical for ethnomusicologists to record the performers of the culture by available means - there are wonderful pictures such as Bartók cranking a machine to record a wax cylinder outside in front of a group of Hungarian singers dressed in festive costumes but looking rather ill-at-ease, and of Frances Densmore recording a Blackfoot chief in the Smithsonian. These pioneers of ethnomusicology have helped preserve styles of music and performance that would otherwise have been completely lost; but it is clear that the very act of the recording creates an artificial situation, especially in the early days of the field, when the recording technology was quite obtrusive. Another related pitfall was the tendency for many of the recordings to be limited to short time durations (such as 10-20 minutes), regardless of the overall duration (the musical event in its entirety might last for hours or days). However, much of the information was contained in verbal descriptions, so for a reader with a good imagination and a good sensitivity to the depth of difference that can exist between one's own culture and another's, it can be extremely valuable. In its maturity, scholars have been able to compensate for many of the shortcomings of traditional methodologies and biases, although there are still major subtle problems, as pointed out by Agawu.[70] On the other hand, modern technologies coupled with aggressive marketing in European and North American popular music industries in particular have produced innumerable instances of "contamination". Some scholars deplore this state, but others argue, fairly convincingly, that this distaste is simply residual colonialism that does not want to allow the "primitives" to evolve their own music. However, there is certainly a case to be made that the Western, especially North American, popular styles and associated marketing techniques have been unnaturally drowning out other voices.

Another major barrier has been the number of musicologists who are not familiar with other languages; for many years, German has been considered essential for any musicologist worth his or her salt, but this does not help in reading ancient texts explaining the intricacies of Persian theory or how this may have influenced European music through the Moorish occupation of Iberia, for example.

ELECTROACOUSTIC MUSICOLOGY - a fairly new and generally not well-known field, composed mainly of composer-musicologists (as Landy, one of its pioneers, points out[71]). I spent a couple of decades of my research-sharing time with this group, and find them full of inventive

---

70. Agawu, 2003.

71. Landy, 1999.

and insightful research. There has been a general ignoring of electroacoustic music by other musicologists for decades, partly due to the often vastly different aesthetic presented in 'ea' concerts but also partly due to the lack of conventional notation. The visual "notation" that often accompanies electroacoustic music is generally a record of the sonic output, rather than a set of instructions to a performer. In the (increasingly frequent) case of music where there is a live component to the music, there may be traditional notation, but often also improvisation. Therefore, there can be crossover between analyses of these works with analyses of jazz and other music where improvisation plays an important part. Additionally, software developed to facilitate analysis in graphic form in the absence of a traditional score has proved to have suitability for other types of music.[72]

POPULAR MUSIC STUDIES - Musicology applied to popular music is often closely related to ethnomusicology, as the context and function are often sufficiently different from the "norm" [Western European 18-19th century traditions of 'art music'] that it becomes necessary to delineate how they are different. On the other hand, much of the work by music psychologists is so firmly based in simpler tonal works that their findings are easily transferred to popular music, which is then reinforced by their use of popular music to help reach a wider base of subjects within their university communities for experimental research. (The prevalence of such simple tonal examples is perhaps based on the erroneous grounds that once we understand them, we can proceed to more complex works, but more likely stems from the fact that several music psychologists had a few years of conservative classical piano repertoire as teenagers before majoring in psychology.)

MUSICOLOGY OF MUSIC+ - Music+ ("music plus")

---

72. See for example Couprie's *IAnalyse*

is my own shorthand for music used in some form of multimedia: music+moving image (film, TV, video); music+dance; music+theatre; music in art installations; etc. So far, there is scarcely a "field" to examine these, either as a group or individually; also, those who are examining music in intermedia / multimedia are often from the 'other side' such as visual arts, and therefore not presenting their findings in a format familiar to 'old school' musicologists. Most visual artists - with the notable exceptions of kinetic art, process art, and earthworks art - still do not seem to consider temporal elements as crucial to their work - nor have studied music or sound design, and this impairs their ability to frame observations about temporal art in general. The field of "music+" shares a lot with ethnomusicology (and popular music studies) in that the function and context are very important. There is also some overlap with electroacoustic musicology due to the common feature of music in such combinations often existing solely on a pre-recorded track broadcast over speakers, rather than being played live. However, the impact of music on visual and vice-versa is clearly something that requires focussed study even to determine what is involved and how the study could be effectively organized (see *Appendix D*).

PERFORMANCE STUDIES - a field emerging over the last few decades that claims to embrace various ways of looking at performance of music as well as other arts, but still tends to be largely populated by people grounded in disciplines relating to theatre. Presumably it could be improved by an invasion of musicologists; the issues are often carefully considered and intelligently grouped. It is worth acknowledging that this is an indication of a paradigm shift, as it implicitly acknowledges that there are many ways of looking at things.

(PERFORMANCE AS) RESEARCH IN PRACTICE could be seen as linked, at least conceptually, with Performance

Studies. One of the essential aspects of this area is that it advocates interspersing periods of non-verbal and non-analytical creative exploration with verbal and reflective periods in order to further an understanding of art and related areas. These can then be analyzed (perhaps by a different person). This whole area seems to run somewhat parallel to the growth of interest in oral histories, where reporting is learned to be valued even if lacking a formal academic dress.

NEW MUSICOLOGY AND OTHER FIELDS – according to Wikipedia, "New Musicology is a non-integrated movement in the musicology field, and it is influenced by feminism, gender studies, queer theory, and postcolonial studies". I am not sufficiently familiar with the nuances of these various fields to attempt a more detailed assessment, as my own efforts to explore them led to the recursive problem mentioned at the start of this book – each contribution seemed to relate to a previous one, and I ran out of time and patience to wade through the various references and dialects of each. Nonetheless, these all clearly belong within any comprehensive guide – although more elapsed time and distance might be useful to distill them into more easily accessible piles. Meanwhile, it seems that many of my complaints about traditional musicology have already been articulated in these areas, so I will rely on others to comment on the degree of overlap.

APPENDIX B

ELECTROACOUSTICS:

MAPPING THE FIELD

The term electroacoustics is used in this book to refer to all compositions that rely heavily on computers, synthesizers, digital manipulation of live or recorded material, etc. for part or all of their predominant sound; in other words, music that integrates the technology into the design, and which is usually characterized as being impossible to imagine as played exclusively on known acoustic instruments. In the early days, many pioneers also enjoyed achieving the sense of no human performers involved – and an absence of human emotion; more recently, the introduction of gestural controllers into music creation has helped provide stunning examples of the contrary – the human performer (often solo) in control of extraordinary sonic / rhythmic palettes used in old-fashioned dramatic effect.[73]

There are other terms that can substitute, or partially substitute, for 'electroacoustics' when used by certain people or in certain contexts: sonic art, electronic music, computer music. Electronic music traditionally referred to a practice of composers who created sounds electronically, by building them up from simple tones generated by oscillators, or by filtering 'noise'. Musique concrète refers generally to the creation of music by manipulating recordings of 'real' sounds, often from non-musical contexts (water, trains, birds, etc.). As these recordings were originally made on wire or more commonly on reel-to-reel tape, both were

---

73. A few of the early electronic gestural controllers such as the Theremin also tended towards a magnification of quasi-vocal expression.

sometimes referred to as 'tape music'. Computer music used to be differentiated from "tape music" in that some composers used the computer for producing or processing sounds, whereas others worked directly with sounds recorded on tape. Now that almost all sound recording is done digitally, the differences have blurred, though the approaches are still quite distinct in character.

It should also be noted that some composers (e.g. Xenakis, Reich, Risset) have used computers to calculate certain elements (such as complex rhythms) for acoustic works that most of us would tend not to consider 'electroacoustic'. On the other hand, some composers imbue their acoustic works with what some might term an 'electroacoustic' aesthetic – sound shapes evolving in time, without discernable melody, for example. But it is not clear that such an aesthetic did not exist in centuries preceding the technology.

It has occasionally been argued that any CD, for example, can be considered 'electroacoustic' because of electronic reproduction; however, that is generally considered a weakening of the term's usefulness. I like the term 'sonic art' to suggest the very abstract use of sound dissociated from the concert hall (into galleries or more public spaces); but it has gathered a particular usage in Britain that interferes with such application; as a result, Landy has proposed the term of 'sound-based art'.

There are increasing numbers of fully-integrated multimedia pieces in the art world (i.e. not just pastiches), and due to the typical technological components, many of these contain electroacoustic music / sound design. However, this still seems to be a category that lives in the cracks between performance studies, electroacoustics, and other cognate areas – which makes it an ideal field for designing, collaboratively, new strategies and perspectives.

APPENDIX C

A TOOL KIT FOR MUSIC ANALYSIS

Dr. R. Mountain, cartographer

The project is envisioned as having two parts:

a GUIDEBOOK explaining the context and acting as a 'checklist' for the analyst who wants to reflect on his/her own stance or for the reader who wants to reflect on the analyst's stance; *and*

a personal database, or a communal wiki, that would be constructed by users interested in submitting 'tips' and hunches on what aspects of which pieces are interesting food for study. In addition, clear examples of musical terms (gesture, non-linear passage, etc.) could be suggested. The tips and hunches would be generally linked to available analyses, but could be simply ideas. (The whole project could easily be linked to current information retrieval sites.) Submitters would normally identify themselves, so if a subsequent user had respect for a certain contributing performer, conductor, or musicologist, for example, those ideas could have considerable weight. See Ch. 5 for more explanation.

A TOOL KIT FOR MUSIC ANALYSIS

outline of proposed contents:

Part A – GUIDEBOOK & CHECKLIST

I. INTRODUCTION

Concept of the Tool Kit; contributing influences; future plans & potential developments.

II. WHAT IS MEANT BY ANALYSIS?

- describing vs. dissecting; centrality of aural, written, graphic, or traditional knowledge;
- measuring intention of composer to effect on listener

III. WHAT IS THE MOTIVATION FOR THE ANALYSIS?

- (performer) improving performance of a particular piece / style
- (composer) studying particular techniques
- (historian / musicologist) study of styles, forms, genres
- (theorist) discovery of underlying principles / adherence to conventions
- (marketer) what makes it appealing?

IV. WHAT IS BEING ANALYZED / FROM WHAT SOURCE?

- fragments or compositions? one or several?
- using what source(s)?
  - ° score (traditional or graphic) /performance instructions
  - ° graphic: (e.g. generated from recorded sonic results)

° audio: recorded / live / remembered

V. What is the piece's original function / context?

- to what extent do we understand the original function / context?
- is it being considered in its original or in alternate contexts, or both? (How) does the analysis reflect / clarify this?
- if the music is part of a multimedia piece (e.g. dance, film), is analysis of the ensemble integrated? envisioned?

VI. What are the main characteristics / features of the piece?

- type of formal structure (simple/complex, traditional model, multi-layered, etc.)
- instrumentation / texture (large ensemble, brass, etc.)
- main activity level of main feature(s) (very slow/very fast, microscopic, etc.)
- which parameters are emphasized (e.g. timbre)
- what is the range of parametric treatment? (e.g. monotone, sine-wave type fluctuation, complex periodic, aperiodic, etc.)

VII. To what depth is the analysis being made?

- temporal focus, the zoom level, hierarchical levels of focus
- is the difference between scales (e.g. form vs ornamentation) acknowledged by the analytical method / in tune with our perceptual grasp?

VIII. How does it reflect temporal scale?

- Is the duration of the piece acknowledged as standard or deviating from average for the genre? Is the genre familiar to the analyst / receiver?
- to what extent is the analysis of the passage/ piece isolated from its larger context? are any crucial elements of the large-scale form lost / unacknowledged?

IX. HOW WILL THE ANALYSIS BE PRESENTED?

- formally / informally
- aural / written / hybrid
- verbal / audio / graphic / multimedia / hybrid
- who is the intended audience? how well are they known by the analyst?
- are there acknowledged or unacknowledged collaborators? corroborators?

X. WHAT METHOD OR STRATEGY IS BEING USED?

- parametric analysis:
  - ° pitch-based - harmony, melody, pitch aggregates
  - ° rhythm - durational patterns, motives, phrase structure, etc.
  - ° form
  - ° timbre (spectromorphology, articulation, instrumentation)
  - ° textural
  - ° gestural
- semiotic / language models / rhetoric
- stylistic / contextual analysis
- social / political analysis (historico-cultural)
- associative: mood / imagery / behaviour
- multimedia-based (performance studies / film studies / dance / art)
- other
- combination of two or more

PART B – REFERENCE DATABASES

I. LIST OF SELECTED MUSICAL COMPOSITIONS & ARTWORKS INVOLVING SOUND – *(with recommended analytical strategies and links to analysis)*

- searchable by title, composer, genre, parameter, etc.
- text fields, and whenever possible, graphics, audio, etc.

II. LIBRARY OF ILLUSTRATIVE MUSICAL FRAGMENTS:

- gestures, textures, rhythmic patterns, temperament, etc.,   searchable by:
  ◦ title, composer, quality, function, etc.
  ◦ text fields (source, dates, descriptive keywords, etc.)
  ◦ and when possible, with audio, graph of sonic result, etc.

III. LIST OF PEOPLE & ORGANIZATIONS:

- researchers, societies, institutes, foundations, etc.

IV. BIBLIOGRAPHY:

- journals, websites, books, articles, etc.

PART C - APPENDICES

Indices - (subjects, terms, titles, names, charts, etc.)

Glossary

Miscellaneous [editorial team / how to contribute, etc.)

Appendix D:

IMP-NESTAR:

INTERACTIVE

MULTIMEDIA

PLAYROOM

- A

NETWORK OF

EXPLORATORY

SPACES FOR

TEMPORAL

ARTS

RESEARCH

IMP-NESTAR is a project invented in 2001 by Rosemary Mountain, and designed in conjunction with her partner Harry Mountain. It was originally named *The Multimedia Thesaurus,* and focussed on a large physical grid framework and small objects with wireless links to computer for sound and image to allow users to "sort" short sounds and images by perceived similarities (whatever those might be), to reflect on useful verbal descriptions for them, and to investigate to what extent people might perceive certain images and sounds as being well-linked.

The project appeals to psychologists as well as musicians and multimedia artists, and appears to be addressing important issues in the area of both music analysis and multimedia creation. It was subsequently extended to the creation of a larger environment, named the *Interactive Multimedia Playroom* (IMP) that kept the basic structure of the original project but included other aspects (books, simple musical instruments, other sorting structures, etc.) to help encourage more discourse on the subject. We began to explore the logistics of reproducing the central framework in various places with real-time links between them.

The project then seemed to expand in various directions, and was recognized as having relevance for subjects as diverse as translation studies, marketing, science museums, and education of emotionally- or intellectually-challenged children. A more recent phase emphasizes the focus on the original areas of music and cognate arts, with the incorporation of both the distributed-space aspect and the network of researchers involved. In this manifestation it is known as *NESTAR – Network of Exploratory Spaces for Temporal Arts Research*, with IMP-NESTAR as the nickname for the global project.

The project has been on hold for a decade due to lack of funds and energy, but is currently being revived.

More information can be found in an old 40-page illustrated booklet and even older video, on the website with new developments to be added as they evolve:

<WWW.IMP-NESTAR.COM>

Bibliography

Please note: This bibliography includes only those books and articles that I have alluded to directly within the text. The reader who wants to know more about my many scholarly influences is urged to look at the bibliographies in my dissertation and previous articles (further details on my website <www.armchair-researcher.com>) as well as my book *A Musician's Guide to Time*.

Agawu, Kofi. 2003. *Representing African Music: Postcolonial Notes, Queries, Positions.* New York & London: Routledge.

Arnheim, Rudolf. 1971. *Entropy and Art: An Essay on Disorder and Order.* Berkeley: University of California Press.

Berry, Wallace. 1976. *Structural Functions in Music.* Englewood Cliffs, N.J.: Prentice-Hall.

Bregman, Albert. 1993. Auditory Scene Analysis: Listening in complex environments. In S. E. McAdams and E. Bigand (eds.) *Thinking in sound.* London: Oxford University Press.

Broyles, Michael. 2000. Metaphors of Chaos and the New Music History. Paper presented at *Toronto 2000: Musical Intersections.*

Chion, Michel. 1990. *L'audio-vision. Son et image au cinéma.* Paris: Editions Nathan.

Clarke, Eric F. 1987. "Levels of structure in the organization of musical time", *Contemporary Music Review*, vol. 2/1: 211-238.

_____. 1989. "The perception of expressive timing in music" in *Psychological Research*, June 1989, Volume 51, Issue 1: 2-9.

Clarke, Eric F. and Nicholas Cook, eds.. 2004. *Empirical Musicology: Aims, Methods, Prospects.* Oxford: Oxford University Press.

Cooper, Grosvenor & Leonard B. Meyer. 1960. *The*

Rhythmic Structure of Music, Chicago: University of Chicago Press.

Erickson, Robert. 1975. *Sound Structure in Music.* Berkeley: University of California Press.

Fraser, J. T. 1982. *The Genesis and Evolution of Time: A Critique of Interpretations in Physics.* Amherst: University of Massachusetts Press.

Godøy, Rolf Inge. 1997. "Chunking in music theory by imagined sound-producing actions." Paper presented at the 3rd Triennial ESCOM Conference, Uppsala University, Sweden.

Godøy, Rolf Inge and Marc Leman, eds. 2010. *Musical Gestures: Sound, Movement, and Meaning.* New York & London: Routledge.

Hope, Cat. The Future is Graphic: Animated notation for contemporary practice. *Organised Sound.* 2020. 25(2):187-197.

Janecek, Karel. 2020. *Foundations of Modern Harmony.* Transl. by Anne Hall & Jana Skarecky [original Czech version1965]. Waterloo, Canada: Wilfred Laurier Press.

Johnson, Mark. 1999. "Something in the Way She Moves". Keynote speech, Conference on Musical Imagery, *6th International Conference on Systematic and Comparative Musicology*, Oslo, Norway.

Juslin, P.N & John A. Sloboda (eds.). 2001. *Music and emotion: Theory and research.* Oxford University Press.

Kramer, Jonathan. 1988. *The Time of Music: New Meanings, New Temporalities, New Listening Strategies.* New York: Schirmer Books.

Krebs, Harald. 1987. Some Extensions of the Concepts of Metrical Consonance and Dissonance. *Journal of Music Theory* 31/1: 99-120.

Landy, Leigh. 1999. Reviewing the musicology of

electroacoustic music: a plea for greater triangulation. *Organised Sound*, 4/1: 61-70.

Lerdahl, Fred and Ray Jackendoff. 1983. *A Generative Theory of Tonal Music*. Cambridge: MIT Press.

Ligeti, György. 1960. "Pierre Boulez: Decision and Automatism in Structure Ia" in *Die Reihe* 4: 36-62 (translated from the original German edition of 1958).

Mithen, Steven. 2005. *The Singing Neanderthals: The Origins of Music, Language, Mind and Body*. London: Weidenfeld and Nicolson.

Mountain, Rosemary. 2001. Composers & Imagery: Myths & Realities" ch. 15 of *Musical Imagery*, Lisse: Swets & Zeitlinger. 271-288.

_____. 2004. Marketing strategies for electroacoustics and computer music. *Organised Sound* 9/3: 307-314.

_____. 2020. Elaborating analogies of time perception. *Organised Sound* 25/2: 259-268.

_____. 2022. *A Musician's Guide to Time*. Self-published.

Nattiez, Jean-Jacques. 2001. *Music and Discourse: Toward a Semiology of Music*. Transl. Carolyn Abbate. Princeton, NJ: Princeton University Press.

Norman, Katherine. 2004. *Sounding Art: Eight Literary Excursions through Electronic Music*. Aldershot, UK & Vermont, USA: Ashgate.

Parncutt, R. 2007. "Systematic Musicology and the History and Future of Western Musical Scholarship" in the *Journal of interdisciplinary music studies*, spring 2007, 1/1: 1-32.

Rudi, Jøran. 2013. "Soundscape as a social construct." Talk presented at EMS-13 (*Electroacoustic Music Studies*), Lisbon, Portugal.

Russolo, Luigi. 1913 (1967). *Art of Noise*. Translated by R. Filliou. Great Bear Pamphlet.

Schafer, R. Murray. 1977. *The Tuning of the World*. McClelland and Stewart.

Schneider, Albrecht (ed.) 2008. *Systematic and Comparative Musicology: Concepts, Methods, Findings*. Frankfurt am Main: Peter Lang.

Slonimsky, Nicholas. 1953. *Lexicon of Musical Invective*. Coleman-Ross.

Smalley, Denis. 1986. "Spectro-morphology and Structuring Processes", in Emmerson, S. (ed.) *The Language of Electroacoustic Music*, London: Macmillan: 61-93.

Tenney, James. 1988. *Meta+Hodos & META Meta+Hodos*. Oakland: Frog Peak Press.

Truax, Barry. *Acoustic Communication*. Ablex, 1984.

Wanderley, Marcelo M.& Marc Battier (eds). 2000. *Trends in Gestural Control of Music*. Paris: IRCAM Centre Pompidou.

Xenakis, Iannis. 1987. Xenakis on Xenakis. *Perspectives of New Music*; 25, 1/2.

_____. 1989. Concerning Time. *Perspectives of New Music*; 27/1: 84-92.

Yeston, Maury. 1976. *The Stratification of Musical Rhythm*. New Haven: Yale University Press.

Zaplitny, Michael and Iannis Xenakis. 1975. Conversation with Iannis Xenakis. In *Perspectives of New Music*, Vol. 14, No. 1: 86-100.

www.ingramcontent.com/pod-product-compliance
Lightning Source LLC
Chambersburg PA
CBHW021228090426

42740CB00006B/439